W0017790

STUDIES IN ROMANCE LANGUAGES: 13

Women in the Medieval Spanish Epic & Lyric Traditions

Lucy A. Sponsler

THE UNIVERSITY PRESS OF KENTUCKY

ISBN: 978-0-8131-5468-8

Library of Congress Catalog Card Number: 74-18939

Copyright © 1975 by The University Press of Kentucky

A statewide cooperative scholarly publishing agency
serving Berea College, Centre College of Kentucky,
Eastern Kentucky University, Georgetown College,
Kentucky Historical Society, Kentucky State University,
Morehead State University, Murray State University,
Northern Kentucky State College, Transylvania University,
University of Kentucky, University of Louisville, and
Western Kentucky University.

Editorial and Sales Offices: Lexington, Kentucky 40506

Contents

Chapter One

The Position of Women: Feudal Europe & Spain

The culture of medieval Spain was anything but homogeneous. It varied not only through time, with the approach of the Renaissance, but also geographically, with great differences between north and south. One significant aspect of any culture is the role taken in it by women. In this study the role of women in relation to men, family, and social organization will be examined in the light of the evidence of literature; the various personalities and types created will be analyzed and their originality within literary convention assessed.

We will try to determine what variations and major changes occur in the role of women in the epic and lyric traditions within the medieval period, and an attempt will be made to relate such changes to what is known of historical, sociological, and cultural trends of the time. First, however, let us glance briefly at the ethnic and cultural background of Spanish women in medieval Spain.

Since wars were so frequent during the feudal period, one suspects that the wife of a noble vassal in any European country must have been thrown a great deal on her own resources. Her husband's obligation of military service to his lord often led him off to battle, and a year's absence was not unusual. During his absence the wife was regarded as her husband's representative and also continued to have charge of domestic affairs. Thus ladies of the minor nobility settled disputes among the servants or peasants, supervised bread-baking, weaving, candle-making, and meat curing.[1] For entertainment some women played the harp and sang troubadour songs. A woman could break the castle routine by riding or hunting. Another activity would have been going out to give alms to aid the poor. Some active women even played a role in reforming corrupt religious orders.[2]

Bourgeois women often had specific trades: they were teachers, weavers, embroiderers, or even merchants who helped in their husbands' stores.[3] Peasant women did not have this much independence. Marriage was the aim of most, but on the wedding night the bride and groom owed the lord not only gifts but the traditional *droit du seigneur*. Only sometimes could a serf purchase exemption from this rite. There were other duties the peasant woman owed to her lord. To bake her bread, for example, she was required to use the lord's oven and to give him a fixed proportion of the loaves as a fee. The same sort of requirement was made for pressing grapes and milling flour, merely one example of the methods used by the lord to preserve his dominance over the peasants. The peasant husband, furthermore, maintained himself in a superior position to his wife, as we can perceive from the story of the peasant who beat his wife on the head every morning, ostensibly to give her something to think about all day. If she were idle, he felt, she would think of evil things, but this way she could spend the day weeping![4]

Although the noblewoman was certainly freer than the peasant woman, there is a similarity in the attitudes of their husbands toward them. Even the noblewoman was expected to devote her time to the care of her husband when he was at home. She had to make sure his guests had all the necessary conveniences, and sometimes she even undressed and bathed the male guests. Thus to some extent the noble lady was left to her own devices when her husband was away, yet she often resembled a servant in that she was expected to keep things in constant readiness for his arrival and to serve him when that time came.

The view that woman waited to serve man while he was out doing much more active things can be substantiated through a comparison of the types of education they received. Lower class women remained illiterate, of course. Among the upper classes a girl received a more bookish education than a boy from a similar family. The princess, for example, was taught to read Latin, to write in a Romance tongue, to do arithmetic, to know the various herbs used to cure wounds, and to sing and play an instrument (for the entertainment of men). For the young prince, on the other hand, the emphasis was on war and tournament skills along with falconry and other hunting methods. Furthermore, girls were taught how to eat and drink "properly," to chew anise or fennel for bad breath, to drink wine to improve skin tone, to walk calmly, to keep their eyelids low when conversing, and the like.[5] This sort of education indicates that woman was thought of as a passive creature of comfort and pleasure for men, as someone to be admired for her habits, appearance, and talents rather than for deeds she might do.

A further indication of medieval attitudes toward women is the number of medieval writers who mistrusted and despised them. Numerous diatribes against them appear in French *fabliaux* as well as in the *Roman de la Rose* of Jean de Meun. In Spain the current of antifeminism was stimulated by Arab influence, for Arab men mistrusted women and kept them apart as a separate part of their lives. This negative attitude toward women is evident in *El Corbacho* of the Arcipreste de Talavera, and *El Libro de los Exenplos* by Clemente Sánchez de Vercial. Even Saint Thomas Aquinas felt that woman was equivalent to sin and that her role in society should be merely to provide food and drink and preserve the species. Saint Jerome has been termed the "patron saint of misogynists," for he felt that "woman is the gate of the devil, the path of wickedness, the sting of the serpent, in a word, a perilous object."[6] The witch-hunting of the late Middle Ages is a gauge of the strength of antifeminist sentiment.

The extent to which a woman could inherit and rule over property provides a further indication of the way she was regarded by a dominant male society. Since fiefs tended to become hereditary, a lord naturally hoped for a vassal to have sons, for otherwise the heir to the fief might be a grandparent or a woman, neither of whom was capable of providing the lord with military service. It was therefore in the interest of a lord to marry off a widow or young orphan daughter of his vassal quickly in order to have a man to rule the fief and serve him in battle.[7] Needless to say this often resulted in unhappy or premature marriages. Rarely did a woman have a choice of mate, for marriages were arranged primarily with political, social, or economic considerations in mind.

How much family sentiment and cohesiveness, how much love between spouses could there have been as a rule during the Middle Ages? If women did not marry people but rather lands or titles, it is not surprising that their emotional needs often led them to a secret love life such as is portrayed in courtly love lyrics. Our emphasis on the prevalence of prearranged marriages and absentee husbands obviously does not paint a rosy picture of nuptial bliss for either women or men; one can easily believe the words of Marc Bloch which indicate that "to place marriage at the center of the family group would certainly be to distort the realities of the feudal era."[8]

Often visitors to Spain today comment that life for women has apparently changed little since the Middle Ages. Although an increasing number of Spanish women, especially single ones, are now seeking a career, many still spend their lives keeping house and caring for their husbands and families. A clue to the cause of this homebody spirit must be sought in Spain's past ethnic and institutional blends. Spanish women reflect Spanish culture, a fusion of Iberian, Roman, Germanic, and Moorish strains in varying proportions throughout the peninsula. This accounts for physical differences established among women of different regions by Hispano-Roman times. Women of the north were tall with fair skin and light reddish-brown hair. In the central portion of the peninsula they were shorter and wiry, while in the south they were dark with lively eyes and graceful, sensual movements.[9] These differences were only heightened by the subsequent Germanic and Moorish invasions and are still visible to travelers on the peninsula today.

At the time of the fifth-century Visigothic invasion of Spain, women in Teutonic regions were legally inferior to men and did most of the hard work with the slaves. Small wonder, then, that in Spain Visigothic women were under the domination of their fathers until marriage and then were sold to husbands who demanded absolute fidelity of their wives while retaining their own liberty. Yet women were not devoid of the trappings of femininity, for they used a reddish hair dye, facial makeup, and jewels.

The major role played by vengeance in the Spanish epic has been attributed by many to the Germanic custom of family revenge for an atrocity committed against one of its members. A large, close-knit clan with several generations living under one roof, the early Germanic family protected its members' safety and controlled their behavior. Though a woman might marry and move into the household of her husband's family, her own relatives continued to feel responsibility for her welfare and would protect her in case of harsh treatment by her husband.[10] This brings to mind developments in the *Poema de Mío Cid,* for Rodrigo springs to the defense of his daughters when they are disgraced by their husbands. As we shall see later, other epic poems also give evidence that this Germanic tendency toward strong family ties and vengeance was maintained in Spain during and after the Visigothic invasions.

The seven centuries of Arab domination influenced Spanish woman-hood perhaps more than any other single factor. Though Arab women were forbidden by Moslem law to marry Christian men, intermarriage between Arab invaders and Christian women as well as forced con-cubinage and slavery brought some Christian women into a polygamous family situation.[11] The harem was a bustle of activity while the hus-band was out, but a silence was enforced whenever he was at home; a wife was considered a humble servant who talked to her husband with respect. When guests were expected the husband received them in rooms apart from the women, whose presence was not requested—quite in contrast to northern Spain where women were expected to receive guests and make them feel at home. In the harem, however, a wife's activities were so rigidly controlled that she was allowed outside only once or twice a month. When she did venture forth she had to cover herself entirely, with the exception of her eyes, in order to avoid arous-ing the attention and desires of other men. Why this should be neces-sary is not clear in view of the fact that Arab men were permitted four wives of their own (purchased often with the aid of a matchmaker); furthermore they were allowed to have female slaves who did house-work and also partook of the husband's bed. Merely by expressing such a desire three times a man could divorce any wife, but a discontented wife had to appear before a judge and, often, buy her way out of an un-satisfactory marriage.

Thus among the Arabs of Spain women were considered a man's possession and were kept in seclusion as much as possible. Apparently they were viewed principally as instruments of comfort and amusement for men, for they dedicated many hours to their "toilette," their baths, unguents, and perfumes, their long hair brushed with ivory combs, their depilatory paste. They used all sorts of cosmetics and chewed gum to sweeten their breath. They wore brightly colored veils and luxuriant silk wraps. Adornment with jewelry, one's own or rented, was widespread; its popularity is reflected in the frequent mention of jewels in the *kharjas*.

It seems clear that women in Moslem Spain were confined yet in-dulged, dominated yet pampered. Intellectual life, nonetheless, was not completely restricted, for there were women who wrote poetry, es-pecially of an erotic and satiric nature. Indeed, with the advent of schools and the study of law, medicine, and astronomy in Moslem

Spain between the eighth and twelfth centuries, women were encouraged to study and often became secretaries and scribes.[12] All in all, though, it does appear that the Hispano-Moslem women led a confined existence and that in men's eyes the ideal life was to be surrounded by innumerable women who retained their youthful, sensuous beauty and neglected their minds. Many men today would, no doubt, still maintain this as an ideal, but in Moslem Spain it was the rule, not the exception.

One tends to conclude that in the north the life of Christian women and the attitude of men toward them form quite a contrast to the situation in the south, for most sources abound in praise of the Christian woman of this period, indicating that she was forced to be a strong, hardworking, long-suffering creature because of the constant insecurity of wartime life. One must suspect an element of Christian bias here. Sánchez-Albornoz contrasts the "sensualidad fácil y luminosa, quietismo, ineficacia, apartamento de la vida del espíritu y de la vida pública" of the Hispano-Moslem woman to the rugged life of the northern woman who lived in a more severe climate and was constantly being forced from her home and having to do without material pleasures.[13] He feels that the kind of life she was compelled to lead promoted a more rigid morality. Yet this particular contrast might be more a result of religious differences between the two sections of the peninsula. Broader implications about the difference in attitude toward women between the two societies stem from the fact that while in the kingdoms of northern medieval Spain women reigned as queens (as we shall see in epic poetry), such could never be the case in Arab territory.

To this day in Spain one notices possible effects of different cultures in north and south. The life-style in the north is certainly more vigorous than that in the south—whether because of climate or because of the contrasts between the customs of north and south during the formative years. Let us look to literary evidence for an understanding of these contrasts.

Chapter Two

Women in Epic Poetry: Law versus Literature

Most students reading the *Poema de Mío Cid* notice nothing surprising in its depiction of the relationship between men and women. Jimena and Rodrigo are deeply in love and happily married. Through the pages of the *Poema* Jimena emerges as an ideal wife, whose deep respect, love, and obedience to her husband stimulate the admiration of the poet and the reader. Epithets such as "muger ondrada" or "menbrada" continually indicate that the medieval poet respects Jimena's prudence and understanding, her virtue and moral qualities.

There is a certain formality in the relationship of Jimena and Rodrigo as portrayed in the poem. Rather than being frivolous and showy, their love is deep and more covert. Rarely is emotion shown by an embrace, and words of love more often than not are words of mutual respect. The fact that Jimena consistently kneels before Rodrigo when greeting him reflects a control of outward emotions and a preference for privacy in expressing conjugal love. There is no doubt of their mutual admiration if we judge from the scene of separation at the convent. Jimena pronounces a long and beautiful prayer for her husband (330-65)[1] and the Cid illustrates equally clearly his sadness at having to leave a woman to whom he is devoted:

> "Ya doña Ximena, la mi mugier tan complida
> commo a la mie alma yo tanto vos queria."
> (278-79)

The emotion of the moment is summarized by the poet: "Assis parten unos d'otros commo la uña de la carne." Equally powerful and moving is the scene of their reunion in Valencia, for the Cid dresses in his finest and parades before his family on horseback (1585-90) to show them his pride and happiness at a reunion under victorious circumstances. As they embrace and weep the Cid shows that his wife and family are a part of his being:

> "Vos doña Ximena, querida mugier e ondrada,
> e amas mis fijas mio coraçon e mi alma."
>   (1604-5)

On the other hand, there can be no doubt that the main aim of the poem is the glorification of a masculine hero, and in achieving this, woman, from a modern standpoint, is viewed in a subordinate and submissive role. Always humble when dealing with Rodrigo, Jimena at one point prefers to kiss his hand as a vassal to a lord rather than to embrace him:

> El Çid a doña Ximena ívala abraçar
> doña Ximena al Çid la manol va besar.
>   (368-69)

Jimena's submissive position is repeatedly revealed through her constant deference to Rodrigo's opinions and her need to rely on his judgment. Rodrigo does not consult with her in the arrangement of the two marriages of each of their daughters, and Jimena does not question his decision to comply with the king's plan to marry them to the Infantes de Carrión. Neither does she question his battle plans at Valencia, but rather accepts whatever he thinks best and concerns herself principally with her responsibilities as a mother, maintaining family unity by remaining with her daughters at all times.

Although Jimena's femininity emerges in the *Poema* through her protective feelings toward the man she loves and trusts, she receives no physical description and is not portrayed primarily as a sex object, a fact which would please our contemporary feminists. Still, nothing she herself does as a character brings her to center stage in the narrative. When Jimena does participate in the action it is often for the purpose of giving Rodrigo encouragement before battle. As he prepares for combat in Valencia in the presence of his fearful wife, Rodrigo reminds her: "Creçem el coraçon por que estades delant" (1655). Rodrigo becomes more valiant when she watches him, wanting to do his best before the woman he loves and respects. Later he invites his family into his new realm, stressing that he has won it for them:

Entrad comigo en Valençia la casa
en esta heredad que vos yo he ganada.
(1606-7)

Jimena can bask in Rodrigo's reflected honor and glory, and she can inspire him to great heights by being present to buttress his masculine
pride; yet these are secondary roles dependent on a man for their fulfillment. Rodrigo respects and loves Jimena because she is a devoted
mother and because she appreciates his masculine strength and valor,
but he and the poet clearly view the ideal wife as lacking any role outside the marital and family structure.

The medieval laws and customs which reveal woman's place in
society, her rights within marriage, and the attitudes of men toward her
corroborate the role Jimena plays as dutiful, but passive, observer. The
previous chapter deals with some of these customs and regulations, particularly those relating to the education of women. In Spain, at the
time of marriage a husband customarily gave his wife *arras* or gifts of
approximately one-tenth of his goods, lands, or horses; this was considered a means of purchasing power over her.[2] However, Alfonso el
Sabio's thirteenth-century *Código de las Siete Partidas* decreed that
during the period of a marriage a wife could not make use of the very
gift her husband had given her (4.11.7).[3] The *Partidas* further provided
that the husband was in charge of the wife's dowry and of all profits
derived therefrom. Hence a medieval Spanish woman was forced to
obey her husband even with respect to the goods she herself had
brought to the union.

Although women could inherit property,[4] upon the death of their
husbands their right to remarry was controlled by limitations on inheritance. The *Siete Partidas* forbade a widow to marry before a year
of mourning for her dead husband had ended. "Muger que casasse ante
de un año despues de muerte de su marido, no la puede ningun ome
extraño establecer por heredera, nin otro que fuesse su pariente del
quarto grado en adelante" (6.3.5). Such a ruling implies a fear that a
woman might conspire to murder her husband for property, and while
Jimena could not be suspected of such ambitions, the motive for this
law will become clear when the personal traits of several other epic
women are discussed. Another restriction placed on women substantiates previous indications that medieval society did not view the sexes

as equal. The *Fuero Real* of 1255 provided a return of the husband's *arras* to him if his wife died before the marriage could be consummated but after he had kissed her, but the wife was provided with only half the *arras* if her husband died under the same circumstances (3.2.5). Evidently a wife once kissed was worth half as much as a husband in the same situation.

The limited role played by Doña Elvira and Doña Sol in finding mates for themselves illustrates how restricted were the rights the medieval Spanish woman possessed even before she found herself subdued in the marital relationship. In the *Poema* each of the girls enters into two marriages, but in no case does either have any part in the decision. The king's unfortunate choice of the Infantes de Carrión was typical of the custom by which a king or powerful lord rewarded a worthy vassal by designating as his wife a girl who was to inherit a large fief. A lord's own need to arrange carefully the marriages of girls from wealthy families living on his lands was discussed in the previous chapter. Furthermore the arrangement of a match between the daughters of local lords and highborn noblemen could be a means of honoring or rewarding the girls' fathers.

Nor was it customary to wait until a girl was of marriageable age before making a match. The *Partidas* indicate that a contract could be signed by a father as soon as his daughter reached the age of seven (4.1.6). Although most sources imply that the daughter's wishes were not taken into account, the *Siete Partidas* seem more liberal in the matter. The fourth *Partida* provided that the father could not force a marriage upon his daughter nor contract a marriage for her if she was not present (4.1.10), though at seven years of age it is unlikely that she could do anything but consent. A father was permitted to disinherit his daughter for refusal to wed, but only if the chosen husband were completely suitable. On the other hand the earlier *Fuero Juzgo*, based on Visigothic laws, was much stricter, requiring that in all cases a girl had to obey her father. In view of the customs and the other statutes of the time, Alfonso el Sabio, composer of the *Partidas*, appears in the thirteenth century to have been one of the first advocates of women's rights.

However, even the *Partidas* did not change the fact that women were often regarded as pawns in arranged marriages. In the words of one historian describing the medieval situation, woman was considered an object "en cierto modo absorbida en el feudo o en el castillo; forma parte del inmueble, pasa con la tierra a quien ha de poseer la tierra y su consentimiento importa poco."[5] Reactions of all parties to the two arranged marriages in the *Poema de Mío Cid* clearly show that economic, political, and social concerns were the major factors considered. Though he did not have complete confidence in his sons-in-law upon their marriage to his daughters, Rodrigo views their departure for Carrión as an opportunity to demonstrate his acquired wealth by giving clothing, horses, and a large sum of money as a dowry. Not only does his generosity show his great love for his daughters, but it also reflects honor and esteem upon their father. The Infantes de Carrión see Doña Sol and Doña Elvira as objects in a good business deal from which both sides can profit, for they observe that they will marry the girls "a su ondra y a nuestra pro" (1888). "Pro" no doubt refers to the chance of receiving a large dowry from their wealthy father, while "ondra" implies that some of the Infantes' high standing in the social hierarchy will accrue to the girls and their family. Social class awareness is also evident in the second marriage, for Minaya berates the Infantes by indicating that the new marriages of Doña Elvira and Doña Sol to Princes from Navarra will elevate their social standing and win them more prestige than the Infantes have:

> Antes las aviedes pora en braços las dos,
> agora besaredes sus manos e llamar las hedes señores,
> aver las hedes a servir, mal que vos pese a vos.
>
> (3449-51)

In their own reactions to the arranged match with the Infantes Doña Elvira and Doña Sol reveal that women did not immediately think first and foremost of compatibility and a personal bond in marriage. From an examination of medieval laws and customs it is clear that girls were not raised with such romantic expectations, and so it should not be surprising that their first reaction is to note the financial benefits of the marriage: "Quando vos [el Cid] nos casaredes bien seremos ricas" (2195). Hence it seems that within the tradition of arranged marriages the woman was viewed as a means by which a man, whether father or husband, could achieve economic and political aggrandizement as well as increased honor through elevated social status.

This is not to impute crassness or insensitivity to the Spanish na-tional hero, for Rodrigo merely followed a medieval Spanish custom which held honor and social esteem to be extremely important values. In addition, as a vassal he had no choice but to accept the king's arrangement and indeed rejected the burden of decision when he told his daughters, "Bien me lo creades, que el [the King] vos casa, ca non yo" (2204). His doubts prove well-founded, and Rodrigo's response to the tragic affront at Corpes, in accord with the Hispanic concept of honor, illustrates still further how Spanish epic society regarded women as of secondary importance.

While not a set of written, codified rules, the Hispanic concept of honor in the Middle Ages was a congeries of beliefs and customs in accordance with which people judged the social acceptability of others. In most societies some people are honored or esteemed merely because of their social position or professional advancement while others have earned renown through personal virtues. In medieval Spain this second type of honor depended on a man's protection of his family from insult or harm, on maintenance of proper comportment within the family, and on vigorous vengeance in the event that he did not succeed in the first two masculine responsibilities. Most historians agree that this custom evolved under Visigothic influence, citing the racial and class pride of the Goths as well as the fact that in Germanic society vengeance was considered a family duty not just morally acceptable under the law but actually expected.[6] A wife who committed adultery or a daughter who had sexual relations out of wedlock brought total collapse of social esteem and personal pride to the man responsible for their protection until such time as he avenged the deed, usually by violent means. Even if a woman had been forced into such a situation through no fault of her own, or if she had been merely insulted verbally or maligned in some other way, society disdained the male protector and viewed him as emasculated until he achieved retribution and restored his *hombría*, his masculine image. In the instance of Rodrigo's daughters, they themselves are mentioned in the series of accusations and challenges during the trial of the Infantes, but they are not called on to testify and never utter a word.

If other ramifications and examples of this code of honor are examined, it is even more evident that preservation of the honor of men was the central motive behind this medieval Spanish tradition. First of all, it would appear that more was at stake for a man if his wife committed adultery than if she remained chaste while he philandered. While an adulteress could be incarcerated for two years if her husband wished it, an adulterous husband was punished at the discretion of the judge and without publicity at that.[7] Such unequal treatment can also be seen in the *Fuero Real,* for while an adulteress loses the *arras,* there is no mention of punishment for an adulterous husband (3.2.6).[8] In fairness, it must be said that the *Siete Partidas* does treat the sexes equally in the case of adultery, for it states that both parties to such an act can be put to death.[9]

Considering all the evidence, it is certain that the Hispanic concept of honor, ostensibly a means of protecting women and restoring pride and esteem to any person who has been wronged, actually centered on the honor, status, and pride of the male. He was clearly considered more seriously damaged by adultery. If a wife or daughter should be dishonored by force, her honor in and of itself was merely circumferential. The main concern was how the honor of the male protector was affected. This will be evident in several other epic poems.

In view of the codes, statutes, and customs of their time it is not surprising that Jimena is shown to be maternal and humble while her daughters are submissive to the decisions and actions of men. However, a study of female characters in several earlier Spanish epic poems reveals some rather unexpected traits. A case in point is Doña Lambra, a central figure in the *Cantar de los Siete Infantes de Lara.* Since, unfortunately, most of the original epic poem has been lost, one must refer to the *Primera Crónica General* (circa 1270) which contains a version of the original *Cantar* in prose form.[10]

In the version of the *Primera Crónica* Doña Lambra marries Roy Blasquez, a relative of Doña Sancha and her seven sons, the Infantes de Lara. At the wedding a contest is held in which all the young men compete to knock down *tablados* (wooden constructions). When Álvar Sánchez, Lambra's cousin, gives a particularly tremendous blow, his strength impresses her so much that she shouts, "Agora vet, amigos, que cavallero tan esforçado es Alvar Sanchez, ca de cuantos alli son elegados non pudo ninguno ferir en somo del tablado sinon el solo . . . et mas valie alli el solo que todos los otros" (*Primera Crónica* 1:431). It is this final remark which touches off the bitter epic feud. Since the seven brothers are among "todos los otros" they feel that their strength and hence their masculinity and honor have been impugned. The youngest, Gonçalo Gonçalez, responds by breaking the *tablado* and then striking Álvar Sánchez, who has become haughty and full of self-praise at Lambra's compliment. When Sánchez dies as a result of the injury, Lambra loudly proclaims that she has been dishonored at her own wedding, and since dishonor to a woman brings shame to her husband, Roy Blasquez joins in the fray by beating Gonçalo Gonçalez over the head. Although the repeated beatings and primitive violence may seem to reach the point of slapstick comedy, such was not the impression created at a time when any insult to one's honor or *hombría* required violent vengeance.

In contrast to prudent, submissive Jimena, Lambra is quite aggressive in expressing her thoughts and feelings. Her tactless praise of Sánchez reveals little sense of her new family obligations and little sensitivity toward others. After all, her remarks are insulting to relatives of her new husband. Lambra is highly egocentric as well. She feels upset at the death of Sánchez because she considers it a dishonor to herself, but she experiences no sorrow at his passing. "Començo a dar grandes uozes, llorando muy fuerte, et diziendo que nunqua assi fuera desondrada en sus bodas como ella fuera alli" (*Primera Crónica* 1:432).

The brushstrokes which paint the picture of Lambra in the *Crónica* are principally her actions themselves. Like Jimena, Lambra receives no physical delineation in the chronicle, and hence there was probably little preoccupation with her appearance or beauty in the original poem. In passing, but significantly, the chronicle introduces her as "una duenna de muy grand guisa" (p. 431), referring to her guile or cunning and contrasting her to her sister, who is described as "muy buena duenna et complida de todos bienes et de todas buenas costrubres" (p. 431).

There could be no greater contrast to these virtues of her sister than the crude vengeance Lambra plans. The beating her husband gave Gonçalo Gonçalez was apparently not sufficient for Lambra; but she refuses to await, as a trusting wife should, further acts from Blasquez. Upon seeing Gonçalo prepare to bathe his hawk, Lambra avows "Que me pesa mucho si el assi escapar de mi que yo non aya derecho dell" (p. 433). However, when she orders a vassal to slay Gonçalez, she is foiled; the fearful lackey runs to hide under Lambra's skirts, where he is killed by the Infantes. Hypocritically, Lambra reacts in the following manner: "Fizo donna Lambra poner un escanno en medio de su corral

guisado et cubierto de pannos como pora muerto, et lloro tres dias . . .
et rompio todos sus pannos, llamandose bibda et que non avie marido"
(*Primera Crónica* 1:434). Rather than shedding tears for her dead vassal,
she concentrates her lament strictly on herself and the dishonor brought
upon her by this murder right before her eyes. In addition, her final few
words imply that her husband has not properly defended her honor,
though actually she has not given him much chance.

The fact that Lambra sees fit to initiate vengeance herself is evidence
of a disregard for social custom which Jimena would find unthinkable.
Even in the instances in which Lambra does leave retribution to her
husband she does not sit by passively, but rather jumps verbally into the
fray. In the case of the vassal murdered while hiding under her skirts,
she loudly demands vengeance from Roy Blasquez; since he is unaware
of the events leading to the situation, he betrays his own nephews and
causes their deaths. Either way Lambra's demands are eventually met.
The violence and primitive tone of this epic continue to the end as
Mudarra, half-brother of the Infantes, orders Lambra burned, a satisfying instance of poetic justice. Thus Lambra is portrayed as a highly unusual medieval woman, for her feelings, her actions, and her reactions
do not often appear to be the product of the sex conditioning of the
day.

Since Lambra's personality and actions diverge so greatly from the
expected role of a medieval Spanish woman, one might suspect that she
is a rare exception. Yet while she may have been considered a grotesque
figure by those who heard the *Cantar de los Siete Infantes* recited in the
Middle Ages, she is certainly not a unique case. This may be seen by
examining the personality of Doña Urraca in the lost *Cantar del Cerco
de Zamora* through its prose version in the *Primera Crónica General.*
The danger of disputes arising from a dying king's division of territory among his children forms the basic theme of the *Cantar.* Don
Sancho, unsatisfied with the territory he receives from his father, King
Fernando I, demands Zamora from his sister Urraca. In her reactions
to this situation Urraca reveals a new dimension of the role of woman.
In keeping with the treatment of Jimena and Lambra in other epics and
chronistic prose versions, we find no physical description of Urraca in
the *Primera Crónica.* Her actions and reactions reveal a curious blend of
the expected passive traits and some surprisingly aggressive ones. In her

emotional response to Sancho's demands, she seems weak and passive. Upon receiving Sancho's message from his courier, young Rodrigo de Vivar, Urraca begins to weep and wishes that "agora se abriesse la tierra comigo porque yo non viesse tantos pesares" (p. 507). Though there is no reference to possible romantic attachment between the young Rodrigo and Urraca here, it is evident that she is conscious of her femininity in the presence of the young cavalier, as she attempts to win his sympathy and help. So far nothing she has done is out of keeping with the behavior expected of a medieval woman.

Yet Urraca is definitely a fighter who does not succumb easily. Her refusal to give up Zamora is coupled with a threat: "Yo mugier so et bien sabe el [Sancho] que yo non lidiare con el, mas yol fare matar a furto o a paladinas" (p. 507). If one of her loyal vassals had made this threat in defense of Urraca, no one would be at all astonished, but a woman capable of such a statement certainly lacks the submissiveness of Jimena in the *Poema*. Indeed, Urraca's aggressiveness and violent leanings recall Lambra. This similarity is heightened when Urraca maliciously incites her vassal Vellido to murder in much the same way that Lambra encouraged one of her subjects to perform a similar deed. Urraca's open-ended offer to Vellido reveals not only the strong-mindedness of its speaker but also the lengths to which she would go in order to achieve her ends. "Non te mando que tu fagas del mal que as pensado mas digote que non a omne en el mundo que a mio hermano toliesse de sobre Çamora et me la fiziesse descercar que yo non le diesse quequier que me demandasse" (*Primera Crónica* 1:510).

As an unmarried woman responsible for governing a city, Urraca plays the masculine role of a leader surprisingly well. Not only does she defy the custom that women marry, bear children, and rely on masculine decisions and leadership, but she may well believe in free love (a possible implication of her statement to Vellido). These attitudes, especially when combined with such a cunning nature and uncommon drive, were not encouraged in young girls of medieval Spanish society. Even Menéndez Pidal refers to Urraca's "ánimo varonil."[11]

This is not to deny that Urraca possessed feminine qualities. The *Primera Crónica* indicates a certain maternal nature: "El rey don Alfonso . . . catauala en uez de madre et assi la onrraua et guyauasse por conseio della" (p. 495). Yet this role of older sister acting as a substitute mother also supports a view of Urraca as an aggressive woman who tended to impose her own will. Her feeling of responsibility toward Alfonso might have political as well as maternal implications, for having Alfonso's respect might be useful at a later time. Despite possible feminine leanings, Urraca does not follow in the footsteps of secondary female characters such as Jimena and her daughters. Rather than adopting the role of a passive observer Urraca makes important decisions and acts on them. Indeed, there is no attempt to soften her aggressiveness, and, most important, she is not subordinate but the central figure of the *Primera Crónica* version of the epic poem.

In the legend of Count Fernán González the case of the Infanta Doña Sancha is of interest because she is a blend of the two contrasting types of women in the Spanish epic poetry already discussed. To analyze her character it is necessary to examine her actions in the Poem of 1250 in *Mester de clerecía* and in its prose version in the *Primera Crónica General*. As in several other cases, Menéndez Pidal postulates the existence of an earlier popular epic upon which the Monk of Arlanza probably based his more learned version.[12]

The Infanta Doña Sancha bears a certain resemblance to Urraca and Lambra in the frequency with which her actions go beyond the norms of medieval feminine comportment. She appears to be a self-sufficient woman who thinks quickly and goes right to the heart of a problem. This is evident in the quick decision she makes to propose marriage to Fernán González in order to facilitate his escape from jail, after she learns of the Castilian hero's plight. Her straightforward words might at first indicate an egocentric attitude:

> Sy esto non fazedes en la carçel morredes,
> commo omne syn consejo nunca d'aqui saldredes;
> vos, mesquino, pensat lo, sy buen seso avedes,
> sy vos por vuestrra culpa atal duenna perdedes.
> (*Fernán González*, stanza 632)

Not only does Sancha adopt her father's role in initiating the choice of a husband, but her own words to Fernán González indicate that she intends to deceive the king by escaping, for she says to the count, "Vayamosnos luego ante que el rey mio padre lo entienda ca noche es ya" (*Primera Crónica* 1:413).

In actuality this self-assertiveness is merely a means to a worthy end, for, as the Lombard count points out, maintaining Fernán González's imprisonment would be beneficial to the Moors, who might otherwise be defeated by Castilian soldiers under his leadership. Furthermore, Sancha's desire for marriage is truly an affair of the heart, as she indicates to the Castilian hero:

> Buen conde, dixo ella, esto faz buen amor,
> que tuelle a las duennas verguença e pavor.
> (*Fernán González*, stanza 629)

Sancha crosses the boundary between medieval male and female roles on two subsequent occasions. In taking it upon herself to secure her husband's release from his second imprisonment her determination reveals itself in bravery and cunning. Donning the disguise of a pilgrim, she is able to gain access to González's cell where she first gains his release from his chains on the pretext that she will spend the night and keep guard over him. Instead, she exchanges clothes with him and he is able to escape. Rather than enlisting the aid of other vassals, Sancha, a woman of action, takes total charge of the plan herself, as Lambra and Urraca would have done. Yet in no case are her motives the selfishness and maliciousness of Lambra and Urraca but rather the preservation of Christianity in Spain and the security of her marriage. She views her role as that of trying to aid her husband as best she can, even if she must remain in prison as a result. Fortunately her cleverness in speaking to the king enables her to escape prison easily. "Fija so de rey et muger de muy alto varon, et vos non querades fazer contra mi cosa desaguisada . . . et en la mi desondra grand parte auredes vos" (*Primera Crónica* 1:421).

A further incident which reveals Sancha's ability to step into a masculine role is the episode in which an Arcipreste demands to have his way with her. Sancha cleverly manipulates him into a vulnerable position, inducing him to remove his clothing and hence his weapons, on the pretext of satisfying his demands. At this point:

> La infant donna Sancha, duenna tan mesurada
> -nunca omne [non] vyo duenna tan esforçada-,
> [travol' a la boruca], diol' vna grrand tyrada,
> dixo: 'Don trraydor, de ty sere vengada.'
> (*Fernán González*, stanza 649)

Her motives are traditional, for she is determined to defend her chastity and honor. What is so unusual is that she succeeds in her efforts, for usually in Spanish literature women give way before force and it becomes incumbent upon a man to avenge the deed, as happened in the case of the Cid's daughters.

Although Sancha exhibits the masculine determination and drive of Lambra and Urraca in taking on any threatening situation, these situations endanger not her ego but rather her country, her husband, her marriage, and her honor. Furthermore, she shows the tenderness and sympathy toward men so far encountered only in Jimena. Such feelings are evident when she responds to the plea for Fernán González's release by the Lombard count. She remarks to a lady-in-waiting:

> Byen vos digo, cryada, tengom' por malandante,
> de quantos males passa mucho so dend pesante,
> mas venira sazon quel' vere byenandante.
> (*Fernán González*, stanza 626)

In addition, her feminine weakness and devotion to her husband appear when she reacts to news of his second imprisonment. "Cayo amortida en tierra et yogo por muerta una grand piesça del dia" (*Primera Crónica* 1:420). Urraca and Lambra are capable of such a reaction only when they feel sorry for themselves. As a result of her generous and ethical intentions Sancha is greatly revered by her husband's men:

> Infanta donna Sancha, nasçiestes en buen ora,
> porend vos rresçebymos [de] todos por sennora.
> . . . .
> sy non fuera por vos cobrar non lo podieramos.
> (*Fernán González*, stanzas 677-78)

Thus she proves that it is possible for a woman to be assertive and aggressive without alienating others.

A final medieval tale which has as a principal character a woman who goes beyond the limits considered appropriate by the society of the time is the legend of the *Condesa traidora*. Like most of the other epic legends, it began as an epic poem. Partial and quite varied versions of the original poem may be found in the *Chronicle of el Toledano* (1243) and in the

Primera Crónica General, while the earliest mention of the legend occurs in the *Crónica Najerense* (ca. 1160).[13] In this version the wife of Garçi Fernández is pictured as a lascivious woman who will do anything to further her aim of marrying the Moor, King Almanzor. It is Menéndez Pidal's view that her own sexual desires and greed spur her to plot the murder of her husband.[14] By arranging for his war-horse to be improperly fed, she endangers her husband's life on the field. These same passions induce her to attempt to poison her own son, for she fears he will stand in the way of her ambitions.[15]

In the version of the later *Primera Crónica General,* an entirely separate aspect of the legend is stressed, for we now read about the period when Garçi Fernández had sought vengeance against his first wife, who had run off with a Frenchman. Once again we have a situation in which the honor of a man hinges on the actions of a woman. The means by which Fernández avenges his honor involves the assistance of the daughter of the French count with whom his wife has fled. Fernández and the daughter murder his wife and the count and subsequently marry. It is this second wife who eventually betrays him and becomes the Condesa traidora whose subsequent actions are described above on the basis of the *Crónica Najerense.*

That the dishonor caused by his wife's desertion is strong enough to provoke murder should not be surprising in view of the medieval codes of law regarding adultery. What is surprising is the role of the consort's daughter in murdering her own father and, later, in betraying her new husband. The Condesa's aggressive, malicious actions can be compared with those of Lambra and Urraca. Furthermore, like the Infanta Doña Sancha, the Condesa seeks her own husband without her father's intervention. When Fernández accepts her offer, she reveals herself to be a woman of cunning and guile, planning her father's murder by herself, and merely using Fernández to implement the plan. Secretly they enter the bedroom of his runaway wife and the count, and the condesa takes charge: "Metio al Conde Garçi Fernández armado de un lorigon con un gran cuchiello en la mano, so el lecho en que amos avien de yazer [her father and Fernández's wife] . . . et defendiol que non se meçiese nin tosiesse fasta que ella le tirase por una cuerda quel ato al pie" (*Primera Crónica* 1:428). This action, combined with her subsequent betrayal of Garçi Fernández, shows clearly that the Condesa's drive for vengeance took precedence over the expected female concern for family unity and marital devotion. Betraying her father and, later, her husband, the Condesa's own interests and desires prevail over any respect or affection. She appears as a much stronger figure than either of the two men, who seem like sheep following a leader. Indeed, the Condesa manipulates men. By the end of the *Primera Crónica* narration, when she is forced to drink the poison she prepared for her son, there is no longer doubt that the Condesa is not only the supreme example of the evil, egocentricity, and ambition found in several women of the Hispanic epic, but that she is totally devoid of any feminine vulnerability or dependence.

If Jimena and her daughters represent the major role played by women in maintaining conjugal love, family honor, and cohesion in the medieval Spanish epic, it is clear that none of the four characters just analyzed fits this image. However, it is equally clear that these four do not fall into a new stereotype opposite to Jimena. Indeed, each displays a unique combination of traits, though all share a certain degree of self-assertiveness and even maliciousness. In contrast to the portrayal of women in the later courtly love movement none of the epic women is viewed with emphasis on her desirability as a sexual object. Nor is there the lengthy psychological probing of these women common in the ballads, for such is not the nature of epic poetry. In the epics these women are not complex personalities but rather have simple passions and ambitions. Except for Jimena all refuse dependence on men and all forego the duties and responsibilities of motherhood. While Sancha, Lambra, and the Condesa do not reject marriage, they repudiate subservience to their husbands and assert themselves as equal to men within and beyond the marital bonds. Doña Sancha is the most mellow of the group, for she manages to persuade others and to control events around her without arousing anyone's enmity or making a fool of her husband. Indeed, hers are the only motives similar to Jimena's—devotion to a man and preservation of her family. The Condesa is perhaps the most malevolent of all, though Lambra provides strong competition. Both, in the end, receive poetic justice, an indication that as historical characters they may have alienated those responsible for creating their legends. The uniqueness of these women will be placed in perspective by an analysis of how they change in the subsequent chronicles and ballads.

It is indeed curious why women who behave the way Lambra and the Condesa do should appear in medieval epics, not only because of the domination of much of subsequent Spanish literature by male heroes but particularly because their roles contrast so strongly with the impression one receives of woman's place in medieval society on the basis of legal rulings and social traditions. It may be that these women became the subjects of stories precisely because they were such exceptions to the general norm. Another possible explanation is the rigor of life in early medieval Spain. The constant fighting often left the women of northern Spain on their own and bereft of material comforts. Gonzague Truc describes woman's situation during the Reconquest in this manner: "En esta sociedad guerrera y austera, la mujer hubo de contribuir a la empresa común no con gracias amables sino con virtudes heroicas. Fue hija, esposa y madre de soldado; compartió las fatigas del varón y sus riesgos; contribuyó, en fin, a virilizar el espíritu de la raza hispana."[16] Although their *virtudes* can certainly be questioned, it may have been such an atmosphere which led some Spanish women to the self-sufficient aggressiveness and dominance over events already noted in epic poetry. The social refinements achieved with new leisure time in the twelfth-century courts of southern France were not cultivated in Reconquest Spain until later. Hence these changes, reflected in the courtly poetry of Provence, did not affect the portrayal of women in the earlier Spanish epics. Women such as Lambra and the Condesa may mirror the harsh, primitive environment in medieval Spain, while the more refined, domesticated portrayal of woman in the *Poema del Cid* may reflect the fact that the *Poema* was composed at a later date than the original epic versions of the other legends.

It is likely that male authors or minstrels portrayed these female characters with some exaggeration in order to achieve a didactic lesson for women of their day. We will probably never know how far these characterizations are true to reality or to plausibility and how far they exemplify the tendency for literature to go beyond reality for dramatic effect.

Chapter Three

The Continuing Epic Tradition

For many years the evolution of the Spanish historical ballads (*romances históricos viejos*) has been the subject of heated dispute. Though the "individualists" believe that each of the historical ballads published in early sheets (*pliegos sueltos*) was composed by one author and remained fixed, Menéndez Pidal and his followers sustain the "neotraditionalist" theory. Pointing to the fact that only nobles of leisure had time to listen to the long epic narratives, neotraditionalists maintain that minstrels for this reason began to modify the lengthy epics. So far our discussion of epic women has centered on original epic poems or on their versions in early chronicles such as the *Primera Crónica General*. In reading later chronicles, for example that of 1344, one soon discovers variations in the original epic material. Menéndez Pidal notes that these later chronicles record the changes which the original epics underwent during the thirteenth and fourteenth centuries, as society became less interested in hearing of military exploits. Particularly evident are changes in the portrayal of women.

In addition, the neotraditionalists maintain that during the period when the epics were being modified a process of fragmentation was also under way so that by the fourteenth and fifteenth centuries minstrels were reciting short compositions dealing with only one dramatic incident from the changing epic poems. Called ballads, these fragments were short enough to maintain the attention of common men and were also easily remembered and passed along from person to person once the minstrel had moved on. They undoubtedly were the preferred passages of the longer poems and were considered popular domain; faulty memory and impulse to improve developed the ballads in directions further and further from the original incidents they related. In these ballads new elements in the portrayal of women evolve even beyond the changes we are about to analyze in the late chronicles. The relationship and progression of these new developments in epic and ballad certainly point to a preference for the theory of Menéndez Pidal.[1]

In the case of the *Poema de Mío Cid* the version of the *Primera Crónica* was written two centuries after the composition of the poem and does show new developments in female characterization. Although the chronicle retains the original poem's emphasis on honor and family unity, we find that Jimena suddenly plays a larger role in events and that in this role more attention is given to her emotional reactions. In the poem she merely accepted her husband's decision that their daughters should marry; yet the chronicle states that "quando lo ella oyo, mostro quel non plazie" (*Primera Crónica* 2:600). And while from the poem we know she was upset at the ill-treatment received by her daughters at Corpes, in the chronicle her reactions are more detailed. She is shown weeping and described as "mas muerta que biva del grant pesar que avie de sus fiias" (2:613). Furthermore, the chronicle adds an entire part to the epic after the Cid's death in Valencia. In this addition Jimena appears decisive and strong-willed, for she takes charge of the Cid's burial and scolds her daughters for an emotional outburst which their father had prohibited lest the enemy discover his death. Although these additions in the *Primera Crónica* are not major, they do reveal more individualization of Jimena's personality and a closer look at her emotional makeup: the weakness expected of a woman, yet masculine strength.

Quite different from the *Primera Crónica* is the subsequent version in the *Chronicle of 1344*, for this version is based on a fourteenth-century epic poem, the *Mocedades de Rodrigo*.[2] Menéndez Pidal suggests that public opinion in the thirteenth and fourteenth centuries clamored for more information about the lives of epic characters, and he believes that the only recourse of the minstrels was to invent new themes and adventures. In the legend of the Cid the result was the creation of a new dramatic episode dealing with the period before the marriage of Jimena and Rodrigo. The *Mocedades* provides a now well-known fictional encounter in which Jimena demands that Rodrigo marry her in order to restore her honor now that he has killed her father. Moreover, the poem creates new personalities for the heroes. Rodrigo is arrogant and brutal while Jimena joins the other epic women in stepping out of the expected feminine role, making known her desires and issuing demands. The creation in the *Mocedades* of a new Jimena, now a dishonored woman who seeks vengeance, and the new novelesque concentration on the amorous sentiments of the young hero and heroine continue the tendency toward development of new dramatic episodes pertaining especially to woman, a tendency first seen in the *Primera Crónica* version of the Cid legend.

The changes which take place in this legend are, of course, familiar because of the plays of Guillén de Castro and Corneille. Not so well known is the fact that in late chronistic versions of other epics there is a similar trend away from original epic plots toward more fictionalization and new characterization. In the *Primera Crónica* version of the *Cantar de los Infantes de Lara* Doña Sancha, mother of the Infantes, is merely mentioned in passing. In contrast, the version of the *Chronicle of 1344,* also attributed to a second (or revised) epic, creates a large role for her. It stresses her motherly, consoling nature as she adopts Mudarra, illegitimate son begotten of a Moorish woman by Sancha's husband while he was in prison. Sancha is a kind, forgiving woman, refusing to be angry with her husband because in jail there is no (moral) law, she feels. In return for her kindness Mudarra gives Sancha the right to decide on the punishment of Roy Blasquez, betrayer of her seven sons. Thus this late chronicle expands the basic plot of the legend. By focusing on Doña Sancha a subplot is developed around a secondary female character.

The other important epic legend which undergoes change in the later chronicles with respect to the role of woman is the *Cerco de Zamora.* While the *Chronicle of 1344* does not change Urraca's basically aggressive and domineering nature as portrayed in the *Primera Crónica,* there is more development of certain episodes between Urraca and Rodrigo. In the *Primera Crónica* she merely mentioned having been brought up with Rodrigo, yet the *Chronicle of 1344* adds: "E dona Orraca, sua filha del rey, lhe [al Cid] fazia muyta honrra. E esta foy a razõ porque a elle [al Cid] amou mais que nem hũu dos seus irmãaos. E nõ enten- dades que este amor que lhe assi avya fosse por algũa vylanya" (3:298).[3] Furthermore, the *Chronicle of 1344* adds an entire scene in which Rodrigo aids Urraca in her request for an inheritance from her father, suggesting that the dying king take Zamora and other lands from his sons and give them to Urraca and her sister.

In the *Primera Crónica* Rodrigo is clearly on Don Sancho's side in his dispute with Urraca; the addition of this new scene in 1344 shows an affection for Urraca that Rodrigo evidently did not feel in the earlier chronicle nor, presumably, in the lost epic. There is no clearly stated romantic attachment, and the element of youthful romantic love has not yet entered the epic tradition in any of the legends studied up to this point. Nonetheless, the *Chronicle of 1344* exhibits a trend toward invention of episodes and details of character which add to the dramatic nature of the legends of the *Siete Infantes* and the *Cerco de Zamora.* We will find the same trend in the ballad versions not only of these but of several of the other epic legends as well.

It is important in view of later developments in the ballads to understand some possible explanations for the expansion of dramatic episodes and the greater detailing of personality traits which characterize the later chronicles. Earlier we touched on Menéndez Pidal's theory that the history of Spanish epic poetry must include a second period from about 1250-1400 A.D. when new versions of older epic themes were fashioned by singing minstrels who adjusted the plots to fit a popular taste no longer preoccupied with war and battle.[4] The episodes which seemed to please and excite their listeners were elaborated and details were added at points where epic action reached peaks of excitement. Clearly these novelesque additions are examples of this trend.

Menéndez Pidal stresses strongly in his works that the change in epic content closely follows a change in thirteenth- and fourteenth-century European society. There is little disagreement among historians about the gradual stabilization of society in this period. In France the thirteenth century brought man a less warlike atmosphere and more leisure time to enjoy elegance and domestic diversions. This is reflected in literature by the advent of the French courtly romance with its concentration on women and analysis of the emotions of love. Still bearing the brunt of the Reconquest, Spain was slower to change. Yet, it seems plausible that the imaginative treatment of epic plots in the second epics, including larger roles for female characters with stress on the emotional or sentimental, is a literary reflection of a changing society. With the Reconquest concentrated largely in southern Spain by the Middle Ages, interests in the more stable north turned away from the military heroes of an earlier era. The flourishing of literature and scholarship in the court of Alfonso el Sabio is just one reflection of the effects of peace.

The trends found in the second cycle of epics develop further in two epic legends we have not yet discussed because of their non-Castilian origins, late date of composition, and differing tone. Nevertheless, the legend of King Rodrigo and the *Book of Apolonio* are important stepping stones in the changing portrayal of woman from the early epics to the later chronicles and ballads.

The time lapse between the original epic dealing with Rodrigo, the last Gothic king, and chronistic prose versions of the legend is much greater than that between the other epic legends and their versions in prose. In part this is why the extant prose versions exemplify to a great extent the late medieval trend toward novelesque elaboration. Based on a very early historical event, the original epic poem died much before other epics. Its subsequent chronistic revival was then based not on pure Castilian epic or legend but on a mixture of Mozarabic, Arabic, and Christian influences and traditions.[5] Each successive chronicle of a very rich chronistic tradition created new details so that La Cava, the main female character in the legend, emerges as a distinct and well-developed personality. This addition of an increasing number of fictional episodes coincides with the trend already noted in the late chronistic versions of the heroic epic cycles.

According to legend King Rodrigo raped La Cava (also called Florinda), who lived in his court while receiving her education. To avenge this dishonor, her father, living in Ceuta, invaded Spain with Arab armies and caused the defeat of Rodrigo. Immediately, then, we find the recurrence of the Spanish epic theme of honor binding man to woman—in this case father to daughter. Unique in the development of the legend, however, is the changing nature of the chronicles as they progressed in developing La Cava's personality.

Three late chronicles demonstrate this clearly. The *Primera Crónica General* emphasizes the masculine force of the king who took La Cava against her own will. "Tomol el rey Rodrigo acá la fija *por fuerça* et yogol con ella; e ante desto fuera ya fablado que avie el de casar con ella, mas non casara aún" (*Floresta* 1:5).[6] Yet the later *Chronicle of 1344*, as in its treatment of the other epic legends, gives more attention to the physical and psychological portrayal of woman. In a hint of sensuality not found even in other late epic chronicles, Count Illán's daughter is described through the eyes of Rodrigo. "Viole el jarrete de la pierna, e era tan blanco e así fecho que non podía mejor ser" (*Floresta*

1:29). Furthermore, this chronicle intensifies the psychological forces in play between La Cava and King Rodrigo. A large portion is devoted to analysis of La Cava's emotional reactions as Rodrigo demands her acquiescence. "Desde el primer día que la el rey começo a demandar, siempre le ella quiso peor de cada día . . . ca ella era de buen consejo e . . . le non podra fazer el rey cosa que su desondra non fuere. . . . Desto le cresçio [a ella] tan grant pesar en su coraçon que començó de perder su fermosura muy desmesuradamente" (*Floresta* 1:30). Despite the novelesque exaggeration of the last phrase, it is evident that the trend here, as in the chronicles of other epic legends, is to intensify dramatic emotional conflicts in which women are involved.

Rodrigo allows passion to govern his actions. As a proud, egocentric monarch, he no doubt expects any woman in court to submit completely to his demands. In a male-dominated society such an attitude is perhaps not surprising. To King Rodrigo, La Cava is merely an object to be taken, just as Doña Elvira and Doña Sol were to the Infantes de Carrión. Further evidence that men viewed women as something less than their equals is found when La Cava is debating whether or not to write her father about the pressure from Rodrigo. She fears that he will not believe her because "todos los sesudos judgan las mas de las mujeres por malas" (*Floresta* 1:31).

The *Crónica Sarracena*, composed about 1430 by Pedro de Corral, adds a further dimension to the drama of La Cava. The chronistic tendency to increase physical and psychological penetration appears in Corral's lengthy analysis of physical passion. New sensuous details heighten the dramatic tension as Rodrigo watches La Cava and her ladies-in-waiting undress in the garden to their "pellotes apretados, que eran de fina escarlata" so that he can see "los pechos e lo mas de las tetillas" (*Floresta* 1:75). The chronicle explains his attraction to her. "Le fallaba las manos blandas, e tales cuales el nunca las viera a muger" (*Floresta* 1:76). Just as the sensual description has increased since the previous chronistic version, so the confrontation between man and woman is elaborated with psychological details. The dialogue between Rodrigo and La Cava is quite lengthy in this chronicle, detailing Rodrigo's attempted persuasion and La Cava's feigned incomprehension of his motives: "E non le quiso dar e entender que ella entendia que el era su enamorado" (*Floresta* 1:78). Indeed, her responses show La Cava to be a very clever debater, for she continues to argue as if

Rodrigo is merely testing her virtue, opposing such a test because, she says, women are weak and might succumb (*Floresta* 1:80).

It is soon apparent, however, that her arguments about the danger of being found out and her fear of dishonoring Rodrigo's wife, the queen, begin to sound like the excuses of a woman torn between honor and passion. Such an interpretation is supported by her final acquiescence. "[Rodrigo] conplio con ella todo lo que quiso. . . . Enpero tanto sabed que si ella quisiera dar bozes, que bien fuera oída de la reina; mas callóse con lo que el rey quiso fazer" (*Floresta* 1:84). Though it is possible that she remained silent in order to avoid being accused of seducing him, indications seem to point to a final willing submission. Thus in elaborating upon this encounter, the chronicle not only gives La Cava an individual personality but also dramatizes her emotional doubts.

It is evident that the *Crónica Sarracena* has a new tone with respect to woman, for the stress on physical passion and beauty are not found in chronistic versions of other epic poems. This difference will have implications for the ballads. However, we must be aware of the similarities if we are to understand how the chronistic treatment of the legend of King Rodrigo in respect to its portrayal of women is a bridge between the late chronicles of other epics and the ballads. In essence that bridge is built by a culling out of dramatic situations dealing with honor and physical passion in which increased analysis of a female personality and emphasis on emotional vacillation are evident. In these episodes, the chronicles of King Rodrigo are a step closer to all the ballads than were the late chronicles of other epic legends.

The next epic legend in which we find an early expansion of a woman's role is the thirteenth-century Spanish version of the legend of Apolonio. Although written in the learned *Mester de clerecía* form, this work does have an affinity with the epic chronicles of the same period. Unfortunately the prose chronicle based on an earlier Spanish verse or Latin prose version of the legend has disappeared, for it was contained in the lost Book 5 of Alfonso X's *Grande e general historia* and might have shown a less erudite tone and style than our version.[7] However, a study of the characterization of women in this learned clerical work reveals a transitional stage in the treatment of women between the early epics and the ballads, for it bears similarities to the thirteenth- and fourteenth-century chronistic versions of second epics which we have been discussing.

Without going into the complicated and diffuse plot of the *Book of Apolonio* let us analyze the treatment of its female characters. Of the three principal women, two, Luciana and Tarsiana, are portrayed with emphasis on their femininity and vulnerability. For example, because of her passion for the hero, Luciana falls ill of lovesickness:

> Tanto fue en ella el amor encendiendo
> Fasta que cayo en el lecho muy desflaquecida.
> *(Apolonio,* stanza 197)[8]

Similarly, La Cava supposedly loses her beauty worrying about King Rodrigo's threat to her honor. Both of these are romantic portrayals of women as delicate, helpless creatures, portrayals which resemble the courtly ideal of woman as a love object of fragile beauty much more than the stronger, more aggressive women in the early epics. This is not surprising since *Apolonio* is a work learned in form and tone; its author must certainly have been aware of the changing view of woman in European society and courtly literature, and this awareness no doubt influenced his literary portrayal.

Certain elements are particularly important for our comparison. First of all, the poem delves into the psychology of love in detail. It shows, for example, how Luciana uses her feminine wiles in an attempt to provoke a declaration of affection from King Apolonio:

> Digasme, Apolonyo, el myo buen rey de Tiro,
> en este casamiento de ti mucho me miro,
> si te plaze ho si non, yo tu voluntat requiero.
> *(Apolonio,* stanza 218)

The value of a good marriage is stressed in the poem just as it is in the *Cantar de Mío Cid,* for the poet comments of Apolonio and his wife Luciana:

> Nunca varon ha fembra nin fembra ha varon
> non servio en este mundo de meior coraçon.
> *(Apolonio,* stanza 241)

New heights of feminine accomplishment are attributed to Tarsiana, daughter of Apolonio and Luciana. Lost in a storm, she grows up moving from place to place and finally living in the court of Dionisia and

Estrangilo at Tarsus. An ambitious girl, she studies seriously during this period, so that by the age of twelve:

> Sabia todas las artes, era maestra complida,
> de beltad companyera non avye conosçida.
> (*Apolonio*, stanza 352)

Subsequent revelation of her ability to sing and play the viola certainly place her closer to the courtly ideal of an educated, beautiful, and talented woman than to the other epic women we have studied.

While living in Tarsus, the heroine achieves such wide admiration for her talents that she incurs the enmity and envy of Queen Dionisia, for whom the people have little respect. Because of her jealousy Dionisia, like Lambra, hires a man to commit murder. Luckily a group of thieves saves Tarsiana from death, but they take her captive to the land of King Antinagoras. It is here that we find a parallel between Tarsiana's actions and those of other epic women. When an evil citizen uses Tarsiana as a prostitute, King Antinagoras wants to be the first client. Tarsiana's determination to retain her chastity again brings in the leitmotiv of woman's honor and its relation to man's. Rather than accept her fate the heroine employs all her persuasive capacities:

> Que tu quieras agora mis carnes quebrantar,
> Podemos aqui amos mortal mientre pecar;
> Io puedo perder mucho, tu non puedes ganar,
> tu puedes en tu nobleça mucho menoscabar.
> . . . .
> Omne eres de preçio, si te veyas logrado,
> sobre huerfana pobre non fagas desaguisado.
> (*Apolonio*, stanzas 408-9)

By cleverly appealing to masculine sympathy, vanity, and honor Tarsiana prevails against Antinagoras and against many others as well. Not only does she retain her honor, but she manages to secure payment anyway. Having won his and our respect, Tarsiana is now able to persuade her captor to let her earn money at a more honorable profession— singing and playing the viola.

Tarsiana's means of avoiding dishonor reminds us of Doña Sancha in the *Poema de Fernán González*, for both heroines exhibit a readiness to defend their honor by whatever means they can muster. Sancha used her understanding of psychology to extricate herself cleverly from jail after she had exchanged clothes with her husband to free him. She even resorted to physical violence to defend her honor against the Arcipreste. Thus she preserved her marriage. Similarly Tarsiana is determined to maintain her chastity despite being forced to live as a prostitute. She is able to do this using persuasion and an understanding of male psychology. Both she and Sancha use their feminine wiles to defend and fight for what they value most.

Unique in the *Libro de Apolonio* is the theme of incest. After he has been told of his daughter's "death" by the treacherous Dionisia, Apolonio wanders into the kingdom of Antinagoras. Finding him melancholy, the king asks Tarsiana, who by this time has a reputation as an excellent songstress, to cheer him up. She asks Apolonio several clever riddles to distract him from his grief, and affection grows between them. Such an attachment portends an incestuous love; however, in the end, as daughter and father discover their true identities, we find that their love becomes familial devotion. Indeed, Apolonio's deep affection for his daughter brings to mind this same feeling as it appeared in the *Poema de Mío Cid*.

We have already noted the evil leanings of Queen Dionisia. Not only does she instigate the murder of Tarsiana but then, believing the deed to be done, she sends the perpetrator away without his promised reward. Her wicked, envious nature contrasts to the ideal qualities of Tarsiana and her mother Luciana, and she bears a resemblance to Urraca and Lambra. In the end as the latter ladies do, Dionisia receives poetic justice; she is burned at the stake.

Thus we see a definite similarity between the *Book of Apolonio* and the early epics in the themes of honor and chastity, wifely love, and the tendency for women to assert themselves in the defense of their own interests, whether for good or for evil. Yet the work shows an affinity to chronistic versions of second epics in its somewhat idealistic portrayal of the heroine, in the view of woman as an object of physical love, and in the stress on her emotional reactions and internal motivations. None of these aspects appear in early epic portrayal of female characters.

An analysis of the traditional historical ballads (*romances viejos*), which evolved in the fourteenth and fifteenth centuries, reveals both a resemblance to the original epics and a continuation of chronistic trends. Most important, we will find new emphasis and direction as well. Since the ballad as a genre tends to be brief and dramatic rather than descriptive, it usually deals with people involved in action situations. The tendency in second epics to add dramatic episodes to the original epics is also evident in the ballads and has affected their characterizations, for rather than merely describing events, the ballads portray characters who react in a dynamic and often emotional manner and who express themselves in rapid, intense dialogue.

In the traditional historical ballads of the Cid, family unity and vengeance of grievances (both values stressed in the early *Cantar*) remain important social considerations.[9] To avenge her father Jimena attempts to turn the wheels of justice upon the man who killed him, as is recounted in two ballads: "Grande rumor se levanta . . ." (*Flor nueva*, p. 121) and "En Burgos está el buen rey. . ." (p. 122). Later in the ballad chronology ("En los solares de Burgos" [*Flor nueva*, p. 131]) she is upset at the king's constant need for Rodrigo in battle, which takes him away from home and family. These typically feminine reactions to the breakup of the family because of the continual strife in medieval Spain could easily belong to the Jimena we met in the epic. Rodrigo also maintains attitudes which he showed in the *Cantar*, saying of the Arabs he has defeated:

> Ni para mis barraganas/sus hijas he de tomar,
> que yo no uso mas mujeres/que la mia natural.
> (*Flor nueva*, p. 155)

Thus the epic reverence for honorable treatment of women is retained. However, the gradual development of the legend away from the early epic and in the new direction of more highly dramatic conflict is seen in the relationship of these ballads to the fourteenth-century *Mocedades de Rodrigo*. Both in this poem and in the ballads the principal events occur at a time before the marriage of Jimena and Rodrigo and center on dramatic personal confrontations.

Yet there is a totally new emphasis which distinguishes the ballads from the chronistic version of the *Mocedades*. Almost all the traditional ballads of this cycle put the spotlight on Jimena, and her outspoken, forceful reactions give her personality new depth. Her desire for retribution, expressed in the *Mocedades* as a fairly calm request for marriage, now takes the form of an energetic, personal demand to the king:

> Justicia buen rey, te pido/y venganza de traidores,
> asi se logren tus hijos. . . ./
> que aquel que no la mantiene/de rey no merece el nombre.
> *(Flor nueva,* p. 121)

No longer is this the seldom-seen Jimena who played a supporting role to the Cid in the *Cantar;* she now bears the central focus of attention. In asking for Rodrigo's hand in marriage to absolve her grief, she takes her defense, a traditionally masculine responsibility, into her own hands. Such a change in her original character must be a creation of the later minstrels, a creation in response to the curiosity and interest of the public about women. It may also be a reflection of a liberalizing trend in society's attitude toward women, for the thirteenth-century *Siete Partidas* certainly accorded her more rights than the earlier *Fueros.* Perhaps, then, Jimena's outspoken role in the ballads reflects a greater freedom in women's actions by the late Middle Ages.

The increased interest in woman as such and her greater role in the ballads as compared to the epic are also revealed in the presence of a physical description of Jimena. Nowhere was her appearance described in the *Cantar* or in later chronicles. However, in the ballads her hair is disheveled *(Flor nueva,* p. 121) as she appears before the king, and at the time of her second demand for justice the ballad describes her mourning clothes as "paños de luto, tocas de negro cendal" (pp. 121, 122). Furthermore, there is quite an elaborate description of her wedding apparel *(Flor nueva,* p. 128). What could more clearly indicate a new interest in the femininity, refinement, and elegance of women than details of wardrobe? For the first time in the legend of the Cid we find a view of woman as someone whose physical presence and beauty are admired. Certainly the social changes mentioned earlier must have played a role in creating this new viewpoint. However, it is essential to realize that the portrait of woman in the Cid ballads is definitely not a courtly stereotype; this is absent from most of the traditional historical ballads, as we shall see.

In the ballads, after their marriage Jimena does become Rodrigo's beloved wife, as she was portrayed to be in the epic, but she is not submissive; rather, she asserts her feelings when, pregnant, she appears before the king to make her plea and to cajole him into allowing her husband to leave the battlefield and restore the unity of their home. It is the forceful, impassioned plea of a self-assured woman:

> ¿Qué ley de Dios vos otorga/que podais, por tiempo tanto
> como ha que fincais en lides,/descasar a los casados?
>
> (*Flor nueva*, p. 132)

Her actions toward her husband when he is going to court to defend his daughters reveal the continuing theme of Hispanic family closeness. Yet at the same time these actions show anew that Jimena has become more self-assertive with respect to her husband:

> No aceteis del rey Allonso/excusas, ruegos ni dones . . .
> Considerad nuestras hijas/amarradas a dos robles . . .
>
> (*Flor nueva*, p. 171)

Menéndez Pidal indicates that these ballads do not appear until the *Romancero General* of 1600. Indeed, Jimena's almost domineering attitude and the superior rather than respectful tone she uses in talking to the king and to her husband would tend to show that they are late ballads, probably of the sixteenth century. Women of earlier epochs had certainly not achieved the status necessary for such freely spoken expression of desires.

If in the ballads of the Cid we find evidence of more interest in woman's appearance and actions, this trend is seen developed further in ballad cycles which evolved from other epic poems. We have already noted that a motherly role is developed for Doña Sancha in the 1344 version of the legend of the Infantes de Lara, whereas in the earlier chronicle she was merely mentioned in passing. The ballads continue to expand her maternal devotion to her sons, as when she spontaneously expresses her love on seeing them:

> Huelgo de veros a todos/que ninguno no fallaba,
> y mas a vos Gonzalvico,/prenda que yo mas amaba.
>
> (*Flor nueva*, p. 95)

This is the first sign of openly and vocally expressed feminine affection in the epic tradition, and both her husband and her adopted son

Mudarra show an awareness of these tender feelings. They wish to avenge the death of the Infantes, not only for themselves but for Sancha, as her husband reveals when he sees his dead sons:

> ¡Hijo Gonzalo Gonzalez
> los ojos de doña Sancha!
> ¡Que nuevas iran a ella
> que a vos mas que todos ama!
> (*Flor nueva*, p. 105)

His love for her and understanding of her emotions is clear to us because she is constantly on his mind. The same is true of Mudarra, for as he kills Ruy Velazquez he expresses his personal thoughts of Sancha for the first time in the versions of this legend:

> Aqui moriras, traidor
> Enemigo de doña Sancha
> (*Flor nueva*, p. 108)

Thus, with respect to Sancha the trend from the original epic to the later chronicles and finally to the ballads is toward a greater outward expression of family affection and compassion. There is no longer the reserve with which family intimacy is shown in the *Poema de Mío Cid*. In addition, there is a new empathy between man and woman, appearing as a masculine desire to protect woman from torment and tragedy.

Turning now to Doña Lambra in the *Chronicle of 1344* and in the ballads, there is a new emphasis on physical love in her reaction to the great strength and ability one of the vassals shows at *tablados*. The chronicle says that Lambra: "Non vedaria su amor a ome tan de pro si non fuere pariente tan llegado" (*Romancero tradicional* 2:109). It will be recalled that in the *Primera Crónica* she admired his strength but had shown no aroused passion. The ballad, however, goes even further in this direction than the 1344 version, for here she says:

> ¡Oh maldita sea la dama
> que su cuerpo te negara,
> si yo casada no fuera,
> el mio te lo entregaba!
> (*Flor nueva*, p. 96)

Here Lambra has become much bolder in referring specifically to a
sexual attraction, following the trend seen in other ballads toward
consciousness of woman as sex object.

Made on her wedding day, this dishonorable remark shows that in
the ballads Lambra has lost none of the insensitivity and crudeness she
evinced in the epic. In fact, not only does she bring into question the
masculinity of her new husband and of the Infantes with this remark,
but she also snaps a vulgar insult at their mother:

> Mas calléis vos, doña Sancha,
> que tenéis por que callar,
> que pariste siete hijos
> como puerca en cenegal.
> (*Flor nueva,* p. 96)

Lambra's callous indifference to the feelings of others is put in clear
perspective as we discover that she can wield insults but take nothing in
return. When Gonçalo Gonçalez becomes the first to succeed in knocking down the *tablado* and praises the valor of his own family, she runs
to her husband to demand vengeance from such an "insult." Certainly
Gonçalo's remarks were less offensive than her own, but we should no
longer be surprised at her emotional outbursts. Lambra exaggerates and
distorts the Infantes' remarks, changing them to a formidable affront
to her femininity and social standing:

> Me pornían rueca en cinta
> y me la harían hilar.
> (*Flor nueva,* p. 98)

Furthermore, according to Lambra's twisted account, the Infantes had
also implied that she would be treated as a prostitute:

> Que me cortarían las faldas
> por vergonzoso lugar.
> (*Romancero tradicional* 2:75)

Such dramatization and expansion of episodes taken from the earliest
chronicle reflect the same trend we have noted toward fictionalization
in the later chronicles, leading to the ballads. Noted in several cycles so
far, the increased emphasis on the actions and emotions of women in

the development of the epic tradition is clearly evident in the central role Lambra plays in the ballads of the Infantes de Lara.

A parallel situation exists in the ballads of the *Cerco de Zamora*, for we find that Urraca now plays a greater role than she did in the epic and later chronicles. Her actions in the ballads are consistently domineering and aggressive, while at the same time new episodes and dialogue show her to be more emotional and sentimental than in the chronicles; thus she conforms to our image of ballad women. Disinherited by her father, she is stunned, and her immediate reaction is a threat to blackmail her family by causing them dishonor:

> Irme he yo de tierra en tierra
> como una mujer errada;
> mi lindo cuerpo daria
> a quién bien se me antojara,
> a los moros por dinero
> y a los cristianos de gracia.
> (*Flor nueva*, p. 137)

Here we find the recurrence of the major epic theme that actions against a woman or by a woman against her family endanger the family honor. The innovation, characteristic of ballads, is the fact that Urraca now makes explicit references to physical love (the evidence from the chronicles shows no direct reference to sexual relations).

A further indication of this new element is found in the new ballad episode involving Urraca and Rodrigo. The ballad goes into greater detail than the chronicles, indicating that Urraca feels a jealous love for Rodrigo.[10] Revealing the bitterness of unrequited love, she says:

> Casastete con Jimena,
> hija del conde Lozano;
> con ella hubiste dineros,
> conmigo hubieras estados,
> dejaste hija de rey
> por tomar la de un vasallo.
> (*Flor nueva*, pp. 139-40)

The story of this amorous triangle, developed dramatically in the *Cerco de Zamora* cycle, illustrates the ballads' growing interest in woman's sentimental nature and in her feelings of youthful passion.

The ways of portraying women in the ballads of Fernán González, the Condesa traidora, and King Rodrigo and in the historical ballads cannot be compared without bearing in mind the distinct origins of the two groups of poems. While the *romances viejos* of the Cid, the Siete Infantes, and the Cerco de Zamora originated through oral transmission from the original epic poems (and were recorded in the chronicles at varying stages in the development of the legends), the sources of the ballads of Fernán González, the Condesa traidora, and King Rodrigo are generally agreed to be written. These ballads were composed and written down by educated poets who were familiar with literary stylistic devices, as is apparent from the vocabulary, style, and metric structure of the ballads. Hence they are called learned ballads (*romances eruditos*) and are generally of a later date (fifteenth and sixteenth centuries) than the traditional ballads (fourteenth and fifteenth centuries).

The ballads of King Rodrigo, for example, were almost all composed on the basis of the various chronicles we have analyzed (particularly the *Crónica Sarracena*). In the case of Fernán González, Menéndez Pidal believes the ballads are based not on a lost epic but rather on a late chronicle of 1509 called *Estoria del noble caballero el conde Fernán González*. This text was not available to me for study; however, Menéndez Pidal cites actual phrases culled from this work (*Romancero tradicional* 2:33, 36), and shows how similar they are to phrases in the ballads. Only five ballads of the Condesa traidora legend remain in existence, and again, excellent documentation by Menéndez Pidal (*Romancero tradicional* 2:265-66), shows that they did not evolve orally from early epics but rather were composed on the basis of the version of this legend in the *Crónica general de 1541* edited by Ocampo.

Since the ballads of these three legends are all of the later, "erudite" variety, it should not surprise us that their treatment of women differs somewhat from that of the traditional ballads. The Hispanic themes of woman's honor and its effects on man's honor and masculinity continue to remain important. The new, deeper development of woman's personality, emotions, amorous interests, and physical passions is maintained in these learned ballads as well. However, in several we find extended portraits of women, portraits which more closely resemble the courtly love ideal than the more austere description of women in the traditional ballads. For example, in one of the two erudite ballads about Fernán González in the *Romancero tradicional* the description of the

Infanta Doña Sancha leaves no doubt of her physical attractiveness and feminine charm:

> La infanta/pues era hermosa y complida
> animosa y muy discreta/de persona muy crecida.
>
> (2:31)

Furthermore, her reactions to the suggestion that she work to free Fernán González reveal not a virago but a sensitive woman capable of tenderness and love. No mention at all is made of her *Primera Crónica* threat to leave him in prison should he refuse marriage. And while in the chronicle she almost single-handedly fought off the priest, in the ballad she flees, leaving the job to Fernán González. Subsequently, on seeing a large army of unknown allegiance:

> La infanta tiembla y se muere
> en el monte se escondía.
>
> (*Romancero tradicional* 2:32)

Clearly this portrayal of the Infanta is the most "feminine" ballad portrait so far encountered. Though the trend has been toward the addition of dramatic, novelesque episodes, this is the first case in which a woman is portrayed as totally meek and dependent. The late chronicle which was its source no doubt had the same characteristics.

Since the erudite ballads of the legend of the *Condesa traidora* show little change from the early chronicles, they are not of special interest here. On the other hand, the ballads of King Rodrigo do vary the chronistic treatment of the legend with more emphasis on episodes involving La Cava. Not only do they focus upon and detail her feelings, but they change her chronistic vacillation and final quiet submission to Rodrigo into a dramatic rape:

> Florinda perdió su flor
> el rey padeció el castigo
> ella dice que hubo fuerza
> el que gusto consentido.
>
> (*Flor nueva*, p. 40)

This ballad portrays La Cava as "una débil mujer sola," a tragic figure suffering pain and fear (*Flor nueva*, p. 41). Her shame and anger at dishonor are expressed in a long, conceptual discourse (p. 42) in which she emphasizes her own powerlessness against the king. The very fact that these ballads view woman as weaker and more vulnerable than man is in harmony with the portrayal of Doña Sancha just discussed, and both portrayals surpass the *romances viejos* in their portrayal of woman behaving in the way we have been taught to think of as feminine.

Furthermore, as was the case in the chronicles of King Rodrigo as compared to the other epic chronicles, now in the ballads the physical description accorded La Cava is much more sensuous than any portraits of women in the traditional ballads of oral epic ancestry. In these erudite ballads the voluptuous description reminds one of erudite Renaissance lyric, for Rodrigo admires "su rostro alindado/sus lindas y blancas manos" (*Flor nueva*, p. 39) as the poet describes:

> Su cuerpo brilla tan lindo
> que al de todas las demas
> como sol ha escurecido.
> (*Flor nueva*, p. 40)

Considering the historical ballads as a group, a trend toward a more prominent role for women is evident both in those of popular oral development and in those of more learned, written ancestry. With greater emphasis on domestic rather than heroic conflicts, episodes in which women play a role are developed in detail. The ballad portrayal of several women of the epic legends does not soften their aggressive, often strident personalities. In certain cases, such as that of Jimena, women have become more self-assertive as the ballads detail their actions. Yet in some cases time has added a note of sentimentality: witness how the crude Urraca mellows and becomes submissive in her jealous love for Rodrigo. Though the theme of love as youthful passion was totally absent from the epics, it is taken up by the ballads as they dramatize and elaborate aspects of the epic which seemed to draw popular interest; specifically they begin to acknowledge feminine charm and physical attractiveness. Physical description of women has appeared in the ballads—for the first time in some legends, such as that of the Cid. This description has revealed a new consciousness of woman in a context of physical love, as in the case of Doña Lambra. Thus the ballads have diminished the heroic emphasis in the epics, accentuating instead daily human contact and emotion.

The change occurring in thirteenth- and fourteenth-century society was mentioned earlier in connection with novelesque additions to epic legends in the late chronicles. Further examination of this transition to a less warlike and more leisurely domestic existence leads to the conclusion that the new trends of the ballads in the portrayal of women are closely related to sociological developments. The stabilization of life in the thirteenth century, the reduction of warfare, the growth of commerce, and the increase in leisure created a demand for material goods and comforts which was being answered by craftsmen. European society was moving away from the crude and barbaric in the direction of "civilization" as we know it.

The development of the well-known system of courtly love is related to the humanizing tendency in society. Since woman assumed a central role in this system, as she did in the late chronicles and ballads, it is important to consider briefly how she was portrayed in thirteenth- and fourteenth-century courtly love literature. Significant contrasts with the Spanish epic and its modifications appear immediately. The rigid and rather repetitious concentration on the marvels of golden hair, eyes which changed color with the surrounding colors of clothing, perfect teeth resembling pearls, and skin white as snow is a well-known characteristic of courtly love portraits of women. The literary stereotype not only laid great stress on physical beauty, but seemed to recognize it in a single, unvarying form. Furthermore, woman appears in such literature almost solely as a love object. If we recall the change in the portrayal of woman from the epic poems through the oral tradition to the ballads of such legends as the Cid, the Siete Infantes, and the Cerco de Zamora, it is clear that women are never portrayed in this manner. In the epic this certainly is not the case, as Menéndez Pidal confirms. "La recia voz que cantaba las conquistas, hazañas, bandas y venganzas de ricoshombres e infanzones no sabía reprimirse para susurrar las delicadas intimidades del amor. Los cantares de gesta eran poesía señorial, de guerra y vida pública; el amor se quedaba para la poesía cortés y burguesa."[11]

The greater detailing of woman's feelings and reactions and the recognition of her interest in physical love in second epics and ballads does seem to point to the cult of woman. Yet in the ballads of the Cid, the Cerco de Zamora, the Siete Infantes, and the Condesa traidora there is no description of woman in accordance with courtly ideals, no placing of woman on a pedestal, and only a slight increase in sensuality over the original epics. Most frequently woman still appears not as lover but as wife, mother, or daughter within a family context. It is only in the more erudite of the historical ballads that one encounters true examples of the courtly view of woman, as we have seen in one of the ballads of Fernán González, in the *Book of Apolonio*, and, particularly, in the chronicles and ballads of King Rodrigo and in the *Crónica Sarracena*, where we find a purely courtly concept of woman. The very theme of the legend lends itself to courtly influence; Rodrigo's adoration of La Cava and her rejection of his implorations both are attitudes essential to the new system of love. Although these ballads do not reach the point of idealizing La Cava into a goddess, as later courtly love poetry would have done, clearly the style in which her beauty is described is of courtly origin. The sensuality of the ballad portraits of La Cava is typified in the following sixteenth-century account of her appearance following the dishonor:

> Bañado en sudor y llanto/el esparcido cabello
> el *blanco rostro encendido*/de dolor, verguenza y miedo.
> (*Flor nueva*, p. 41)

The increased intimacy and voluptuousness and a preoccupation with the psychology of passion are characteristic of the courtly attitude toward woman and quite in contrast to any sentimental preoccupation in traditional ballad cycles.

A comparison with the characterization of her contemporary in French literature shows that the portrayal of woman in the popular Hispanic epic tradition is unique. It is important to realize that the French had no truly popular epic tradition, for even the earliest epic poems still extant are longer and reveal a more erudite style and content than those of Spain.[12] Not only did learned influence reach the epic earlier in France than in Spain, but the very nature of this nation's epic was different. As Américo Castro puts it, in the French epic "se le habla al pueblo desde un plano que no es el suyo, y de cosas a infinita distancia de su pobre vida de todos los días."[13] Implicit here is a contrast with the Spanish epic which deals with actions and situations closer to the everyday reality of most of its medieval audience. Small wonder, then, that the view of women in French epic contrasts sharply with what we have seen in Spanish poetry.

In the earliest French epics of the eleventh and twelfth centuries (*Chanson de Roland, Cycle de Guillaume, Raoul de Cambrai*) there is proportionally less attention given to the role of women in the narration than in Spanish epic poems. While the Spanish epic stresses the role women and family play in creating and maintaining a man's honor and masculinity, the French epic views honor as an especially good official job or fief or, even more important, as glory and renown acquired in battle.[14] Honor thus has little to do with the sanctity of the home. With the emphasis on heroic military accomplishment, men rarely think of or mention their women in the French epic. While Aude dies on hearing of Roland's death, he himself had breathed his last "en pensant à son épée, à ses conquêtes et à son seigneur."[15]

On the other hand, to a certain extent the French and Spanish epics share the veneration of woman as devoted wife and mother. Reminiscent of Jimena's devotion to her husband is the reverence Guibourc shows her husband when she greets him (*Chanson de Guillaume*). "Elle lui baise le pied et s'incline devant lui en le recommandant à la bonté divine."[16] In *Raoul de Cambrai* the view of woman as mother recalls Spanish epic. Raoul's mother Aalais reveals the same concern for her son that Doña Sancha shows for her family. Both women share maternal fear of disaster and a fervent wish for their sons not to fight. However, though woman is venerated as a maternal symbol in the French epic, she is encountered infrequently. Thus the family and woman's role in it are never as central a theme as they are, for example, in the *Poema de Mío Cid*.

Furthermore, because the early French epic contains physical description of woman which was totally absent in the early Spanish epic, woman appears as a more feminine creature in the French works. Whereas the epithet "mugier ondrada" was used constantly in reference to Jimena, the portrayal of women in the early French epic, though not of the courtly type, does emphasize beauty, refinement, and even fragility. In the Guillaume cycle, Part 1, we find that Guibourc "fu femme si out fieble la char" (v. 1292), and in Aliscans we find "Aëlis au clair visage" a frequent epithet. Spanish woman, on the contrary, usually appears in connection with a problem of honor, and whether she be aggressive or even wicked in the defense of what she justly or unjustly considers her rights, nevertheless it is her judgment and reactions which are emphasized in the Spanish epic tradition.

It will be recalled that no allusion to physical love was found in early Spanish epics; yet in the French epic there are early references. In the *Chanson de Raoul de Cambrai*, Béatrix loves Bernier and is described as embracing him and attempting seduction (5699). Although Lambra indicated a physical attraction to Álvar Sánchez, no such clear attempts at seduction appear in the Spanish epics. Only in the very late learned ballads (such as those of King Rodrigo) is such passion indicated, and even then not on the part of a woman. Thus even in the earliest French epics, which were contemporary to the Spanish epics and much earlier than the Spanish ballads, one finds less emphasis on woman's role in everyday social and family structure, but more stress on her role in love affairs. The Spanish view of woman in the epic tradition retained its individuality despite a great deal of French influence in the peninsula between the eleventh and thirteenth centuries.

A comparison of the treatment of woman in literature evolving from the French epic and contemporary to the Spanish ballads shows the essential closeness of the Hispanic epic and ballad views of woman, despite the divergences we have noted. While the *romances viejos* remained a popular creation, developing episodes of important action from epic themes, the French epic retained its learned style and had developed complex plots around the theme of courtly love by the end of the thirteenth century. We have seen that the Spanish ballads show more interest in woman, her amorous adventures, and her physical presence, than the epics from which they derived. Yet the romances of chivalry which resulted from the development of the French epic rarely deal either with epic themes or with epic women. The women who do appear are portrayed in a stereotyped manner utterly foreign to traditional Spanish ballads: "Toujours grêle et blanche 'comme la neige' ou 'comme une fleur' avec les 'yeux vairs.'"[17] The only similar descriptions in the Spanish epic tradition are of the elegant, refined women one finds in the late ballads of Rodrigo and in the *Libro de Apolonio,* and both of these are of learned derivation. Most women of the popular, Hispanic oral tradition are not refined, but rather crude and outspoken in expressing their desires and feelings. Love is usually conjugal and private rather than openly passionate like that of the young lovers in the French tradition, and there is essentially little hint of physical intimacy between man and woman in the traditional Spanish ballads.

One cannot help wondering why it is unique to Spanish literature that women increase in importance from their comparatively large role in epic poetry to their very prominent one in the ballads and yet absorb very little of the stereotyped treatment of the day. The fact that the epics and ballads studied here developed through oral transmission indicates that theirs is essentially a popular genre in which the minstrels sang for everyone—for the common man as well as for court nobility. Since the minstrels themselves were of the common people, this most clearly accounts for a realistic rather than idealistic treatment of woman. Where learned literature stresses stereotyped female beauty and woman as an object of love, the more popularly created epic and ballad tradition emphasizes personality development, questions of honor, and the role of woman in conjugal and maternal love. Apparently the popular genius considered woman important enough in daily life that she deserved an important role in literature, a role realistic in terms of the social values of the people living on the peninsula. Apparently, too, this opinion was held by the audiences, since the ballads were created and molded according to their interests.

Chapter Four

Popular & Traditional
Lyric Poetry: The Two Spains

If in the epic poems and chronicles we found that woman had a modest, though slowly increasing, role, we shall find that she plays a central role in popular and traditional lyric poetry contemporary with the early epic poems. Not only will we find her to be thematically the focal point of the lyric, but there will be a difference in the very way she is portrayed. In part, of course, the deviation is related to a contrast between the two genres. While the epic stresses action, usually the domain of man, lyric poetry concentrates primarily on interior feelings, sensations, and emotions; and in daily events women traditionally tend to express such feelings in a less inhibited manner than many men. However, we will see that this is not the only explanation of woman's major role in the popular and traditional lyric poetry of medieval Spain.

It is the widely accepted theory of Menéndez Pidal that traditional peninsular lyric evolved in the same way that the historical ballads did, that is, through the changes arising from the constant repetition of verses passed along from person to person. While the troubadours were devising fixed metrics and standard topics for the poetry they sang in the courts, and while clerics were writing lengthy poems on religious themes, counting syllables and perfecting rhymes, anonymous poets among the populace were forming simple lyrics which would be repeated by others, changing as they spread until they became established folk refrains. The portrayal of woman in this indigenous, autochthonous lyric is the subject of the present chapter.

Literary critics have divided the primitive lyric of Spain into three regional types: the early Andalusian lyric called the *kharjas*, the Castilian primitive lyric, and the Gallego-portugués lyric.[1] Discovered early in this century as short lyrics in the Romance tongue of the Mozárabes placed at the end of Hebrew or Arabic poems called *muwaŝŝahas*, the *kharjas* are now believed to have been traditional mozarabic refrains on which the longer Arabic and Hebrew *muwaṡṡahas* were based. The role of women in the *kharjas* will be extremely important to the conclusions of this chapter.

The primitive lyric of Castile most often appears in the form of a *villancico*, or traditional refrain familiar to the majority of the populace, and a *glosa*, or elaboration of several stanzas' duration improvised by a particular poet; such poetry is called *popular lyric* by Menéndez Pidal and we will employ his terminology, for though the *glosa* is learned, the popular refrain is retained. The anthology edited by Dámaso Alonso and José Manuel Blecua is useful in a study of these Castilian traditional lyrics because it includes numerous examples of the many types: *malmariadas, serranillas, albadas,* and others.[2]

It is more difficult to cull out traditional or popular Gallego-portugués lyric, for the only available sources are copies of the thirteenth-century Galician *cancioneiros: La Vaticana, Cancioneiro da Biblioteca Nacional,* and *Ajuda.* These collections do contain some traditional *cantigas de amigo* (or excellent imitations inspired by the latter). Typically Gallego-portugués is their frequent theme of a girl singing of love and suffering to her mother. Also uniquely Gallego-portugués is their parallel construction.[3] On the other hand, many poems in these collections lack parallel construction and reveal Provençal influence not only in their complex, conceptual style but also in theme. The lyrics of this type are called *cantigas de amor* and deal not with the amorous sentiments of young girls but rather with the suffering which men endure because of their cold-hearted ladies. In a study of woman in Gallego-portugués traditional lyric of the *cancioneiros* one must be careful to base conclusions on the *cantigas de amigo,* those lyrics which are simple in tone and treatment and which portray a woman singing rather than a man, in order to avoid interpreting as popular the characteristics of the *cantigas de amor,* influenced by more learned developments from external sources.

S. M. Stern, the discoverer of the *kharjas* in 1948, has published a collection of approximately fifty of these poems.[4] Although some are fragmentary, certain generalizations may reasonably be drawn about the portrayal of woman in these lyrics.

One type of woman often appearing is the young, inexperienced girl who feels the first awakening of emotional love but is uncertain how she should behave. The imploring *kharja*, "Qué fare, manima? Meu l'habib est'ad yana" (Alonso and Blecua, *Antología*, p. 4), which translates as "¿Qué haré? mamá, Mi amigo está a la puerta," indicates that the girl has not achieved the experience and confidence necessary to make her own plans and relies on her mother as confidante and adviser. One can visualize her in a moment of excitement and timidity as she runs imploringly and uncertainly to her mother. Another girl is evidently just as electrified by the anticipated arrival of her lover, as she reveals this jubilation to her mother:

> No dormiré yo, madre:
> Al rayar la mañana
> (creo ver al) hermoso Abu-l-Qasim
> con su faz de aurora.[5]

Similar sincere and girlish enthusiasm is accompanied in other *kharjas* by concern for the welfare of the beloved, expressed lyrically in such poems as:

> Mi corazón se me va de mí.
> Oh Dios, ¿acaso se me tornará?
> ¡Tan fuerte mi dolor por el amado!
> Enfermo está, ¿cuándo sanará?
> (Alonso and Blecua, p. 3)

However, there are girls who reveal neither excitement, jubilation, nor anxiety, but rather self-assertiveness and self-confidence, as is indicated in this *kharja* translated by Stern: "Je ne veux pas avoir le collier, ma mère, . . . la robe pour moi. Mon seigneur veut que mon cou apparaisse dans toute sa blancheur au dehors, il ne veut pas de joyaux" (p. 13). Clearly this is a girl much less innocent than the one first mentioned, for the lyric implies sensuality and a desire to attract and please her lover as well as to surrender to him. Other *kharjas* will reveal similar characteristics.

Indeed, rather than awaiting the arrival of their lovers, the more mature women of the *kharjas* often seek out their men. Their intense desires make them dependent and force them to show their cards: "Mon seigneur Ibrahim, ô toi, homme doux, viens chez moi, dis-moi ou je te

rencontrerai" (Stern, p. 22). Such initiative in the realm of love occurred in the Spanish epic but only when a woman stepped into the
shoes of her father in arranging her own marriage (cf. the *Poema de
Fernán González* and the Condesa traidora legend). However, in the
kharjas marriage is never clearly part of the relationship. This is evident
in the previous citation, for the use of the word *seigneur* implies that
Ibrahim is in a superior position, a position of authority as compared to
the woman, just as the feudal ruler was to his vassals. It is also clear that
Ibrahim is not the speaker's husband, for if this were so the wording
would probably be "viens chez nous." Hence this lyric seems to imply
an extramarital relationship in which the woman views her male partner
as the superior force.

The tone of numerous *kharjas* supports the assertion of many historians that women in the society of Andalusia during the eleventh and
twelfth centuries were accustomed to willing submission to the rule of
men. Over and over in the lyrics woman appears eager for man's attentions, available for them, unable to think of anything else. In some
poems she cannot sleep without him: "Je ne dormirai pas, au rayon du
matin, bon Abu'l-Qasim, la face de l'aube," (Stern, p. 31) while in
others she wonders desperately what will become of her if he leaves her:
"Qué faré yo o qué seréd de mibi? . . . non te tolgas de mibi" (Alonso
and Blecua, p. 3). Metaphorically she speaks of man as the center of
her existence: "Vayase meu corachón de mib" (Alonso and Blecua,
p. 3), and in a literal sense her remark is true as well, for she has no direction in her life without him, yet with him she is insecure because of
her fear that he will fail her: "Mon Dieu, comment pourrai-je vivre avec
un tel seducteur! Un tel qui, avant de saluer menace déjà de partir"
(Stern, p. 7). In many *kharjas* woman demands loyalty of her lover but
is powerless to keep him: "Va-t'en misérable, va-t'en, car tu ne t'en
tiens pas à ton intention" (Stern, p. 19). This dependence and total
commitment of woman to man is not the conjugal love and trust of
such epic poems as *Mío Cid* and *Fernán González*, but rather an emotional and sensual dependence on man in an insecure relationship.

Earlier we noted in the epic the lack of physical description of
woman and the absence of stress on woman either as an object of male
desire or as a person with similar desires of her own. In contrast, not
only is love in the *kharjas* extramarital and therefore, one would suppose,
implicitly more based on sex, but in many of these lyrics it is treated in

a specifically sensual manner not present in the epic. One representative lyric clearly indicates the physical attraction woman in the *kharjas* feels toward man: "O toi/qui est brun, ô délices des yeux! Qui pourra supporter l'absence, mon ami? " (Stern, p. 20), and elsewhere, "Je ne veux aucun compagnon sinon le brun," (Stern, p. 28). Further: "Ma mère, quel ami: Chupamieles' rouge! Le cou est blanc, la petite bouche rouge" (Stern, p. 29). What each woman chooses to describe are, no doubt, the qualities she finds most attractive about her lover, and in every case the description is purely visual: his coloring and his physical appeal. It is clear that in this type of *kharja* man's allure for woman is expressed in primarily sensual terms.

A further contrast to the portrayal of woman in the epic and traditional ballads is the fact that in the *kharjas* she often takes the initiative in seeking physical love: "Bouche de perles, douce comme miel, viens et donne moi un baiser! Mon ami, viens chez moi" (Stern, p. 57). Indeed, in numerous kharjas woman plays the role of seductress encouraging and appealing to man to enjoy her in a sexual relationship. She even describes her own physical assets in a manner much too lascivious to appear in the epic or ballads: "Grâce, mon ami, ne me fais pas cette querelle! Bon (Homme de bien) baise ma petite bouche; [je sais que?] tu n'iras pas" (Stern, p. 33). Even more sensual is the following plea: "Si tu m'aimes comme un homme de bien, baise ce fil de perles ici, cette petite bouche de cérises" (Stern, p. 27). On the other hand, instead of encouragement we also find woman rejecting man's advances in a specific manner referring to physical love: "Ne me touche pas, mon ami, . . . mon corsage est délicat" (Stern, p. 10). Judging from the tone and content of most *kharjas* this rejection is probably meant to tease and stimulate a man's ardor rather than to cool it.

In all the *kharjas* woman's yearnings and appeals are beautifully lyrical and very moving. Of course they are much too brief to allow for any individual personality traits to be developed. Variation in the principal theme of love revolves around several types: a young girl confiding in her mother and afraid to follow her longings, one who worries for the welfare of her man, a woman dreading abandonment by a lover on whom all her happiness and ecstasy depend, or one who attempts to seduce her lover by revealing her own sensuality and desirability. Except for woman concerned for her man's welfare, none of these types are ever touched on in the epic and traditional ballads. Furthermore, in some *kharjas* woman portrays herself specifically as a physical object for man's sexual gratification, and she herself often shows a conscious desire for physical love; neither of these attitudes appeared in the epic though they were hinted at in the ballads. The desire for physical love in the *kharjas* is usually accompanied by a clear emotional dependence on her part, but no mention is made of woman's importance in marriage or in rearing a family. The *kharja* women wait for each brief meeting, and no potential permanence is ever indicated in these relationships. While they never appear in the lyrics, it is obvious that men of the society portrayed are free to come and go as they please. So although women express equality in their right to sensual fulfillment and in intensity of passion, men are clearly portrayed as superior, for they have a liberty that women lack, emotionally and socially.

Love is also an important theme in the early popular lyric of Castile. Yet in this poetry the basis of love for woman lies as strongly in emotional needs as in physical desires; the extent to which the physical and sensual aspects of love are present in Castilian lyric is not nearly so great as in the *kharjas*. Certainly women make indirect references which show they are aware of themselves as physically attractive to men. One such lady clearly shows this in a *villancico:* "Segúnt vuestra embajada,/ habréis mi cuerpo garrido" (Alonso and Blecua, p. 12). However, unique to these lyrics is the emphasis on a role in life for woman more in keeping with the mores of northern Spain in the Middle Ages as seen in several of the epics. The lyrics to which we shall refer in order to demonstrate this are attested in various manuscripts and *cancioneros* of the fifteenth and sixteenth centuries, according to the research of José María Alín. Yet since these poems are of oral origin or are developments of traditional themes by particular poets who have maintained their popular tone, we can assume that these lyrics date from at least a century or two before their earliest appearance in written form.[6]

Though it went unmentioned in the *kharjas*, married love has a role in the Castilian lyric, as Alín points out in this lyric:

> Soy doncella enamorada,/quiero bien y soy amada;
> si me llaman desposada,/con el m'iré.
> Uno quiero y uno amo,/suya soy, suya me llamo.
>
>   (p. 262)

Of importance here is the fact that the young lady in question says she will go away with her beloved, but only if they are married. Furthermore in Castilian popular lyric we find woman rejecting illicit encounters because of devotion to her husband. In one lyric the refrain indicates that it is out of the question for a married woman to be unfaithful:

> ¿Qué me queréis, caballero?
> casada soy, marido tengo.
>
> Casada soy, y a mi grado
> con un caballero honrado,
> bien dispuesto y bien criado
> que más que a mí yo lo quiero,
> casada soy, marido tengo.
> (Alonso and Blecua, p. 20)

Even in the lyrics of the *Malmaridada,* where woman is cursed with an unhappy union, we still find that the sanctity of marriage is unbreakable, and she is resigned to remaining faithful despite her husband's philanderings. One such poem deals with a cruel husband who provides his wife with neither clothing nor gifts but rather with whacks and beatings, who insists that she stay up at night and indoors by day, yet is unfaithful to her, while she remains loyal:

> Así Dios me preste la vida y salut
> que nunca un besillo me dió [el marido] con virtut
> en todos los días de mi juventut
> que fui desposada.
>
> Que bien que mal, sufro mis tristes pasiones
> aunque me tienten diez mil tentaciones . . .
> (Alonso and Blecua, p. 11)

Apparently such experiences were common enough to cause some women fearing unhappy marriages to attempt escape via the convent:

> De iglesia en iglesia
> me quiero yo andar
> por no malmaridar.
> (Alonso and Blecua, p. 68)

Another example of the Castilian lyric's concern for woman within
the Hispanic moral system is the fact that even when there is no marriage the loyalty of a woman to her lover is repeatedly the subject of
this poetry. Here the relationship of woman and her beloved is never
based merely on physical desire, but rather the implication is always
that the couple intend to marry or at least are faithfully devoted to
each other. For example, one poem deals with the sudden infatuation
of a young girl and her fidelity from that moment on. Falling in love at
first sight she promises her lover three kisses when she grows up and
maintains her pledge:

> Los ojos con que le ví/han seído causadores
> que sean mantenedores/los votos que prometí:
> la promesa que le dí/yo muy bien la guardaré:
> creceré y dárselos he.
> (Alonso and Blecua, pp. 14-15)

Another type of poem, the *cantiga de romería*, deals with a young
girl who goes to a sanctuary to pray for the safe return of her lover
from battle against the Moors. In this type of lyric the girl does not indicate that she wishes his return because of her own physical desire, as
would be typical in the *kharjas*. Rather hers is a sincere concern for the
well-being of a beloved. Other poems reveal a womanly and even
motherly concern for a man's well-being, even if he is not the beloved
of the girl who sings:

> Aquel caballero, madre,
> si morirá
> con tan mala vida como ha.[7]

A further illustration of the differing view of woman's relation to man
in the Castilian lyric is found in a poem dealing with the very problem
of sensuality. A young girl has been "assaulted" by love:

> Temprano quiso saber
> el trabajo e placer
> qu'amor nos faz haber;
>
> . . . .
>
> a los diez años complidos
> fueron d'ella conocidos

todos sus cinco sentidos
. . . .
a los quince ¿qué fará?
(Alonso and Blecua, pp. 12-13)

Here is a clear indication that the society which produced the Castilian lyric frowned upon the overly free indulgence of woman's sensual needs. Certainly passion is a part of love as viewed in these lyrics, but the values of morality, loyalty, devotion, and marriage are more often stressed. Such loyalty, especially in marriage, is clearly related to the fact that infidelity on the part of a wife was a severe dishonor to man and the family name in Hispanic epic society. Since the Castilian lyric poetry of the period stresses related values, this further substantiates our conclusion that conjugal devotion and morality before and after marriage were key elements in society's view of woman in northern Spain of the Middle Ages.

By no means should this indicate that the emphasis in Castilian lyric is totally on woman's ethical qualities to the exclusion of physical ones. As in the *kharjas*, there is certainly more reference to female beauty in the early Castilian lyric than there is in the epic and ballad tradition. However, the sensuality which is present in the Castilian lyric is much more indirectly and subtly expressed. There are only hints of desire and hence a feeling of mystery surrounds physical love in the early lyric of Castile:

No sé qué me bulla/en el calcañar,
que no puedo andar.

Yéndome y viniendo/a las mis vacas
No sé qué me bulle/entre las faldas
que no puedo andar.
(Alonso and Blecua, p. 44)

We have here not the full-blown consciousness of a woman experienced in romance, as in several of the *kharjas;* rather these are the incipient sensations and desires of a young, innocent girl, probably a peasant girl at that, judging by the fact that she tends cows. The poem merely hints at her awakening in a titillating manner rather than in more specific description.

Another poem, similar in tone, deals with an attractive young girl who is probably unaware of the feelings she stirs in men:

> Isabel, Isabel/perdiste la tu faja;
> héla por do va/nadando por el agua.
> ¡Isabel, la tan garrida!
> (Alonso and Blecua, p. 44)

Other poems do refer to more obviously developed physical yearnings of a woman:

> El durmiendo, velo yo,/abrasándome su fuego;
> deste velar me quedó/vida con poco sosiego.
> (Alonso and Blecua, p. 34)

Yet even here there is no explicit depiction of the masculine features she finds attractive, and the treatment of sensual desire is discreet.

Most often if there is an implication of feminine sensuality it is stressed less than woman's simple feelings of affection. One very lyrical poem artfully shows woman trying to conceal her love by inadvertently lowering her eyes on seeing her man:

> Ojos de la mi señora/¿y vos qué habedes?
> ¿por qué vos abaxades/cuando me veedes?
> (Alonso and Blecua, p. 12)

The women of these lyrics clearly want male company, not seclusion:

> No quiero ser monja, no/Que niña namoradica so.
> Dejadme con mi placer,/con mi placer y alegría,
> dejadme con mi porfía,/que niña malpenadica so.
> (Alonso and Blecua, p. 26)

A *serrana* indicates a similar feeling:

> Madre, ¿Para qué nací
> tan garrida
> para tener esta vida?
>
> De vevir muy descontenta
> mi tristeza se acrecienta,

> el alma siempre lamenta
> dolorida
> por tener tan triste vida.
>   (Alonso and Blecua, pp. 28-29)

The implication is that a woman needs a man in an emotional sense as well as in a physical one (¿Para qué nací tan garrida?). Yet not one of the Castilian poems describes in detail a woman's physical desires nor do they give her an opportunity to describe herself as physically appealing to her lover.

Another revealing aspect of the Castilian lyric is the relationship it shows between the mother and the young girl who speaks. In the *kharjas* the girls often merely confided their feelings and intentions to their mothers, while in the Castilian lyric the mother sometimes exercises strong control over her daughter, a control absent from the Andalusian lyric. For example:

> No oso alzar los ojos
> a mirar aquel galán,
> porque me lo entenderán.
> Si a dicha le salgo a ver
> cuando por mi puerta pasa,
> luego me riñen en casa.
>   (Alonso and Blecua, p. 33)

We see here the efforts of a girl to emancipate herself, to break away from the family restrictions of honor in order to achieve the end toward which her youthful urges direct her. Passion has a mind of its own as we see in the following lyric as well:

> Una madre que a mí crió
> mucho me quiso y mal me guardó;
> a los pies de me cama los canes ató,
> atólos ella, desatélos yo;
> metiera, madre, al mi lindo amor:
> no seré yo fraila.
>   (Alonso and Blecua, p. 75)

This final line seems to indicate symbolically a rebellious insistence on having her freedom and pleasure, an attitude unknown in the woman of the epic or ballad.

A theme of the *kharjas* treated similarly in Castilian lyric is female initiative in love-making. In one *albada* a woman invites her lover to visit her: "Amigo él que yo mas quería, venid al alba del día," while in another instance she passionately demands:

> Bésame y abrázame,
> marido mío,
> y daros he'n la mañana
> camisón limpio.
> Yo nunca ví hombre vivo
> estar tan muerto,
> ni hacer el adormido
> estando despierto.
> (Alonso and Blecua, p. 61)

However, this clear female attempt at seduction is within the bounds of a married relationship. In addition, the attempted seduction is not nearly so voluptuously descriptive as a similar *kharja* situation; its depiction of the man is more burlesque than sensuous. In a third case of female seduction a man relates what a *serrana* has said to him:

> Comeréis de la leche/mientras el queso se hace
> Haremos la cama . . ./haremos un hijo.
> (Alonso and Blecua, p. 4)

Again the difference between this seduction and similar situations in the *kharjas* is clear. This shepherdess is not presented as a voluptuous woman. She does not seduce passionately, but rather crudely and specifically, as in a documentary: "Haremos la cama . . . haremos un hijo." Of course her awkwardness and direct, brusque approach are probably related to her peasant extraction. Yet it is important to note the reference to childbearing as the goal of physical love rather than emphasis on carnal pleasure.

Finally, let us remark that in no case in the Castilian lyric is woman shown to be in despair because she is under the domination of man. She may long for his return, but usually he is not pictured as cruel because he has abandoned her, as in some *kharjas*. Usually he is gone not by choice but because of duty, so we do not find woman thinking of man as a false and unfaithful tormentor. On the other hand, there are a few instances in which woman is actually viewed as the tormentor. If she is not cruelly disdainful, nevertheless there are several poems in which she is portrayed as a goddess with man as her servant. These poems bear a resemblance to the courtly love lyrics in which woman is worshiped and may be later poems influenced by the Provençal tradition, though they were supposedly composed by poets imitating popular lyric. For example, the following poem illustrating male devotion clearly places woman in a dominant position, quite in contrast to the other Castilian lyrics and to the *kharjas* as well:

> Perder yo la vida
> podrá ser, por cierto,
> más si sois servida
> contatme por muerto;
> mas no ser incierto
> de viestro querer;
> que no puede ser.
> (Alonso and Blecua, p. 38)

Another brief lyric does stress woman as an object of physical desire, as in the *kharjas*, but it also indicates that she has the ability to wound and thus subdue man:

> Los cabellos de mi amiga
> d'oro son:
> para mi, lanzadas son.
> (Alonso and Blecua, p. 13)

Like Provençal lyric, this poem not only intimates that woman has power over man, but it also uses the common stereotype of Provençal and Renaissance poetry: woman of golden hair.

Another theme of courtly love poetry occasionally encountered in the Castilian lyric is that of a man fearing that his love will be unfaithful. As we noted above, this is rare, for much of the lyric does stress marital devotion or loyalty to one lover only; hence the few instances of male insecurity might reveal external influence. As Peter Dronke points out, both popular and learned poetry were probably recited at mealtimes when the aristocracy was served by the lower classes, and thus some mutual influence was possible.[8] For example:

> ¿De quién habedes miedo
> durmiendo conmigo?
> De vos, mi señora,
> que tenéis otro amigo.
> (Alonso and Blecua, p. 53)

This theme of male suspicion, quite common in courtly love poetry, is the antithesis of the popular lyric view we have encountered in both the *kharjas* and in Castilian lyric, a view which if anything stresses female dependence on man.

Despite these few examples of female superiority and male insecurity which recall conventional Provençal themes, the rare physical descriptions of woman in the Castilian lyric do not present her attractive features in a stereotyped courtly manner; moreover, they are more subtly sensual than those of the *kharjas:*

> Niña, erguídeme los ojos
> que a mí enamorado m'han.
> No los alces desdeñosos,
> sino ledos y amorosos,
> que mis tormentos penosos
> en verlos descansarán.
> (Alonso and Blecua, p. 18)

The concentration on the eyes as an admired feature emphasizes their attractiveness while implicitly characterizing the girl as shy and feminine. In other poems there is little physical description of woman beyond terming her body attractive:

> Encima del puerto,
> Allá cerca el vado,
> vide una serrana,
> del cuerpo lozano;
> sin duda es galana.
> (Alonso and Blecua, p. 75)

In contrast, the women of the *kharjas*, it will be recalled, actually pointed out and described their features most attractive to men: their red lips, shining hair, gleaming white teeth.

In conclusion, we have seen a great deal of variety in the characteri-

zation of woman in the Castilian lyric. Her presence as a sex object for
man is stressed less than her role as a loyal mistress or wife. Though she
is rarely granted status superior to man's, neither is she portrayed as extremely subservient to his domination. And while she does show interest
in the sensual aspects of love, these aspects are not described in detail;
and it is clear that for woman in the Castilian lyric the goals of love, in
general, are companionship, marriage, and children.

The *cantigas de amigo* share with the *kharjas* and Castilian lyric the
theme of the relationship of a young girl to her mother. Yet in treating
this theme the *cantigas* seem to combine the roles given to the mother
in the other lyrics, stressing one or the other. We recall that in the
kharjas the mother was often a confidante, listening silently as her
daughter sang of newfound emotional attachment and desires. On occasion the daughter asked for advice, showing youthful excitement tem-
pered with uncertainty. At other times she merely informed her mother
of her attempts to please her lover, or her intentions to do so, and
asked neither for permission nor help. Yet never was the mother
pictured as objecting to her daughter's wishes in the *kharjas*, though
this was always the case in Castilian lyric. In the Gallego-portugués
lyric the mother appears in both roles. At times she is warmly sympathetic to her daughter's affection for her lover, while her daughter
seems inexperienced and dependent:

> —Que me mandades, ai madre fazer
> do que sei que nunca ben querer
> soub'outra ren?
> —Par Deus, filha, mando-vo-l'ir veer
> e sera ben
> e do que lhi faz voss'amor sofrer
> guarra por en.
>
> (Nunes 2:86)[9]

On other occasions the mother does not speak at all, but rather listens
as her daughter confides the anguish of love:

> Non chegou, madr', o meu amigo,
> e oj'est o prazo passado!
> ai, madre, moiro d'amor.

. . . .
E oj'est o prazo passado!
Por que mentiu o perjurado?
   ai, madre, moiro d'amor.
          (Nunes 2:17)

These poems resemble the *kharjas* rather than Castilian lyric in their portrayal of the mother's attitude toward her daughter's activities.

On the other hand, there are several occasions in the *cantigas* when an attempt is made to control the girl's actions by preventing her from keeping a rendezvous:

   Des que o vi en Julhan un dia,
   já me non leixan, como soia,
   a Santa Maria ir,
   pois mi non leixan ir.
          (Nunes 2:324)

No doubt it is her mother who is primarily responsible for this cautious protection, as in a similar case:

   Mia madre velhida e non me guardedes
   d'ir a San Servando, ca, se o fazedes,
     morrerei d'amores.
. . . .
   E se me vós guardades, eu ben vo-lo digo,
   d'ir a San Servando veer meu amigo,
     morrerei d'amores.
          (Nunes 2:339)

Since this type of maternal supervision is found frequently in both types of regional lyric of northern Spain, it may reflect a stronger moral concern of the family for the actions of a daughter in northern society. The response of the young girl to this parental surveillance is similar in the *cantigas* to that found in Castilian lyric. She often shows rebellious independence from her mother and determination to see her lover, throwing caution to the wind:

   Oje quer'eu meu amigo veer
   porque mi diz que o non ou sarei
   veer mia madre, de pram veer-lo-ei

e quero tod'en ventura meter
e dés i saia per o Deus quiser.
(Nunes 2:106)

In *cantigas de amigo* dealing with more mature passion, as in the Castilian lyric, we find that woman's physical desires, absent from the epic, are now present. However the wording used in their description is again not nearly so sensual as that of the *kharjas*. The following poem will indicate the subtlety with which this sensuality is expressed.

Digades, filha, mia filha velida;
porque tardastes na fontana fria
os amores ei;
. . . .
Tardei, mia madre, na fontana fria,
cervos do monte a augua volvian . . . .
(Nunes 2:419)

Since, as Asensio indicates, the reference to deer going to water is a phallic symbol of biblical origin, we can see that there is an innuendo of sexual ecstasy in the girl's reason for delaying her return from the fountain.[10] Other *cantigas de amigo* have the same implied rather than explicit sensuality:

Madre, moiro d'amores que mi deu meu amigo,
quando vej'esta cinta, que por seu amor cingo.
(Nunes 2:18)

Her statement seems to indicate not physical frustration and annoyance at the chastity belt but rather loyalty to her lover and a burning desire for him alone.[11] Fidelity was a value noted also in the Castilian lyric. In addition, this girl's smoldering passion is merely implied when she says she is dying of love. One final poem illustrates this discreetness:

Non poss' u voss non vejo
viver, ben o creede,
tan muito vos desejo
e por esto vivede
amigu, u mi possades
falar e me vejades.
(Nunes 2:30)

We know precisely what she desires, but the physical is not specifically stressed in the Galician lyric.

The young girl singing of love to her mother or other confidante in the *cantigas de amigo* dwells most frequently on the misery she endures because of her lover. The causes of her suffering reveal further characteristics of woman in the *cantigas*. One of the most typical complaints is that she suspects her lover of lying. The mere refrain

> Que ant'el queria morrer
> ca mi sol un pesar fazer
> (Nunes 2:14)

indicates that her happiness depends on her man and that whereas previously he had done her no ill and caused her no grief, now his attitude seems to have changed. Her dependence is made clear in other lyrics that stress how deeply man can hurt her. One girl complains:

> Pero ouve-m'el jurado
> ben aqui, se Deus mi valha,
> que logo m'enviaria
> mandad'ou s'ar tornaria.
> . . . .
> Mais, pois non ven, nen envia
> mandad, e mort ou mentia!
> (Nunes 2:8-9)

Thus not only is her need physical, as has been implied, but it is also emotional in that she depends on the fidelity of her mate. Indeed, just as in Castilian lyric, the woman of the *cantiga de amigo* values loyalty highly and fears disloyalty:

> Ai fals'amigu'e sen lealdade
> ora vej'eu a gram falsidade.
> (Nunes 2:46)

This suspicion of infidelity also appears in the *kharjas*, but not nearly so frequently as in the *cantigas* and Castilian lyric. Another *cantiga* also expresses the importance of loyalty in the eyes of woman:

> Non vos membra, meu amigo,
> o torto que mi fezistes?

>posestes de falar migo
>fui en e vós non veestes
> e queredes falar migo?
> e non querrei eu, amigo.
> (Nunes 2:78)

In this particular case her reaction reveals unexpected strength and self-assertiveness, for she refuses to speak to him. Whereas in the *kharjas* dependence and subordination were shown by woman's insecurity and fear of desertion, in the *cantigas* it is more a question of her being furious after the deed is done. The submissiveness and despair of woman in the *kharjas* is not reached in the Gallego-portugués lyric.

The *cantigas,* like the Castilian lyrics, portray woman worrying about her man, not through fear of losing him, as in the *kharjas,* but showing concern for him as a human being, as in this *cantiga marinera:*

>Ai eu coitada como vivo
>en gran cuidado por meu amigo
> que tarda e nao.
> (Colocci-Brancuti 2:297)[12]

Another combines the essence of the *cantiga marinera* with the *cantiga de romería:*

>Sedia m'eu ermida de San Simon
>e cercaromi as ondas que grandes son;
> eu atendend'o meu amigo.
>Estando na ermida ante o altar
>cercaromi as ondas grandes do mar;
> eu atendend'o meu amigo.
>E cercaromi as ondas que grandes son,
>e non ei barqueiro nen remador;
> eu atendend'o meu amigo.[13]

The repeated mention of the threatening waves gives an ominous tone to her melancholy and deeply moving lament for his apparent misfortune. The similarity of the attitudes of this woman and of the woman of the Castilian *cantiga de romería* mentioned earlier is quite striking.

The three regional lyrics have in common a central role for women and several thematic elements: the presence of mother or friend; love often causing more pain than joy; and woman's dependence on a man who, she fears, will not return. Yet we have seen that though the themes may be the same, the manner in which they are treated and the resulting role of woman are subject to great variation.

Though we found that the *kharjas* include specific references to woman's beauty, her coloring, her lips ("bouche de cérises") and to her physical expression of affection in kissing and embracing, northern lyric contains only innuendos of sensuality; woman clothes her desire for man in an aura of mystery. Instead she often expresses anxiety over the disloyalty she fears in her mate. Thus woman's love, as revealed in the *kharjas*, seems to have a basis in physical need, while the other regional lyrics give at least equal if not more emphasis to an emotional basis as well. Such a dichotomy in the two presentations of female love is further substantiated when we consider that the *kharjas* show woman as an illicit seductress while in the northern lyric she is equally often seen in the role of loyal companion or wife, potentially the mother of children. Furthermore only the northern lyric shows woman as a mother trying to protect her daughter or to discourage her from possibly damaging involvements at an early age. In both Castilian and Gallego-portugués lyrics woman despairs over her lover's absence or fears his disloyalty; yet the extreme dependence on man shown in the *kharjas* does not appear, nor is man portrayed as a totally dominating force. Thus within similar contexts northern and southern Spain tend to diverge in their popular lyric portrayal of woman.

Yet differences in the treatment of woman do exist between the two regional lyrics of the northern peninsula. In the Castilian lyric there seem to be proportionally more instances where woman appears younger, more innocent, and less worldly-wise in her relations with men than in the Gallego-portugués lyric. We found this in the case of young girls quite unaware of their new physical maturity and its effect on men as also in the case of the peasant girl who brusquely stated her desires to a man in an unsophisticated, forward manner. In addition, Menéndez Pidal notes that although the Portuguese and Castilian lyrics both portray the themes of the mother and the *amigo*, the Castilian lyric rarely mentions the *amigo*.[14] Moreover, there seems to be less emphasis on woman as wife and more situations of illicit romance in the *cantigas* as compared to Castilian lyric. Thus it appears that the Castilian lyric portrays woman in a stricter moral context than the *cantigas* do.

Although the French bourgeois lyric of the period is replete with ridicule of the female sex, negligible satire of woman emerges in the popular regional lyrics of Spain. In our next chapter we shall see that the female sex is not always treated with reverence in Spanish erudite lyric. However, in the popular type of lyric under study here such mockery of woman's physical features or habits is practically non-existent as far as we have been able to determine. Perhaps this lack reflects a certain respect accorded to woman among the common people of medieval Hispanic society, for even though she is portrayed as subordinate to man, respect for her worth as mistress, wife, or mother has been evident both in epic and in popular lyric.

We have assumed that one reason why woman plays a more central role in popular lyric than in epic is the difference in nature of the two genres. Further understanding of the causes of the interest popular lyric takes in women requires some study of the origin of this poetry. Since the *kharjas* are the earliest known peninsular popular lyrics, our investigation must take us to a search for the origins of these poems and of the role of woman in them. The fact that they are in the Mozarabic tongue spoken by Christian peoples under Arab rule has led many critics to theorize the Romance origin of the *kharjas*—that is, an origin among Christian peoples. Both Dámaso Alonso and Emilio García Gómez subscribe to this theory.[15] Alonso feels that Arab poetry is too erotic, even obscene and orgylike, to have inspired the trembling voice of a young girl in love in the simple *kharjas*, much less the chaster Galaico-Portuguese and Castilian lyric. The fact that he is attempting to prove that the *kharjas* are merely *villancicos romances* around which Arab or Hebrew poets built their *muwaššahas* has, no doubt, influenced his thought, for he has neglected to mention that the fearful young girl in love is not the only type of woman in the *kharjas*. We have seen that there were mature women in the *kharjas* who took the initiative and attempted to lure their men in a highly erotic manner.

Indeed, an examination of Arabic poetry on the peninsula prompts the conclusion that its concept and treatment of woman had much in common with that of the *kharjas*. In his study of Arabic poems written in the Andalusia of the eleventh and twelfth centuries, and hence contemporary to the *kharjas*, García Gómez points out that this poetry "rezuma una sensualidad que todo lo impregna de dormida lujuria."

Further on he describes the poems as revealing "una frenética adoración por la belleza física, que es . . . bien característica de la mentalidad musulmana."[16] We have already noted in the *kharjas* that woman tried to attract man through the appeal of her physical beauty. Furthermore, the metaphors used in the voluptuous physical descriptions of woman in the Arab poetry of southern Spain along with the view of woman chiefly as a physical object remind one of the treatment of woman in the *kharjas*, where description of woman's appearance becomes very explicit:

> Era tan blanca que la juzgarías una perla . . .
> Pero tenía las dos mejillas—blancas como el
> alcanfor puntuadas de almizcle.

Another poem is equally voluptuous:

> Su blanca figura avanzó cubierta
> con un vestido de color de la rosa, como
> la luna envuelta en el manto del crepúsculo.[17]

A comparison of such description with that of the *kharjas* bears out the closeness in tone of the two and the greater distance from their treatment of woman to the less sensually specific northern lyric. Such *kharjas* as the following could easily pass for Arabic poetry in medieval Spain:

> Je ne veux pas avoir le collier, ma mère,
> . . . la robe pour moi. Mon seigneur veut que
> mon cou apparaisse dans toute sa blancheur au
> dehors, il ne veut pas de joyaux.
> (Stern, p. 13)

> Si tu m'aimes comme un homme de bien,
> baise ce fil de perles ici, cette petite
> bouche de cérises.
> (Stern, p. 27)

This similarity does seem to support the theory that the *kharjas* were influenced by attitudes of Arabic society.

Could the attitudes of Mozarabic Spain (as expressed in the *kharjas*) have influenced the peninsular lyric of the north as well? Clearly as people mingled and made new contacts during the Reconquest the Christians must have heard Mozarabic lyric recited, and thus the views in such lyric could easily have been incorporated into or at least influenced the songs or refrains brought from the north. Furthermore, Dámaso Alonso points out that at the same time many *Mozárabes* were emigrating northward to Christian lands, bringing their songs and traditional refrains with them.[18] Thus the Arabic attitudes to which we attribute the sensual portrayal of woman and the revelation of her physical desires in the *kharjas* could have reached the Galaico-Portuguese region as well as Castile.

A further point supports this theory. Both Asensio and Alonso point out that the *muwaššahas* of Hebrew and Christian poets show what Asensio calls "una actitud más recatada hacia el amor," when compared to the *muwaššahas* of Moslem poets (which Asensio feels confuse love and sensuality).[19] Such a division within the *muwaššahas* further points to the tendency of Arabic literature toward the sensual treatment of woman, toward regarding her as an object of physical love for man. Hence this distinction strongly indicates that what sensuality we have found in the popular lyric of Castile and Galicia is more likely to be of external derivation than to form part of local folk tradition. The most likely influence would appear to be that of Moorish society.

Before the discovery of the *kharjas* many literary historians, especially those of French background, had tried to prove that Provence was the cradle of European lyric and had exerted a prime influence on all peninsular lyric. This would lead to the conclusion that the Provençal view of woman was an important influence in shaping her portrayal in peninsular lyric. On the other hand, since the *kharjas* have come to light, a number of critics, including Menéndez Pidal, have attempted to show Arab influence as a chief factor in creating not only peninsular lyric but the learned lyric of Provence as well.

Certainly there is no denying the similarities between eleventh- and twelfth-century Arab poetry and the Provençal lyrics of courtly love, the earliest of which date from the late eleventh century. An examination of the metaphors used to describe the beloved in *muwaššahas* and other Arab lyric of Andalusia reveals a close resemblance to descriptions in the Provençal lyric. In both, woman's physical beauty is worshiped as excelling that of all natural phenomena. A comparison of the following translation of an Arab poem with the subsequent extract from a poem by the troubadour Bernart de Ventadorn clearly shows the similarity in adoration of woman:

> Levantó sus ojos hacia las estrellas, y
> las estrellas, admiradas de tanta hermosura,
> perdieron pie, y se le fueron cayendo en la
> mejilla, donde con envidia las he visto en-
> negrecerse.
>
> Ahora no veo lucir el sol, tanto se me han oscu-
> recido sus rayos; y no desmayo por ello,
> porque una claridad me solea de amor, que me
> ilumina dentro del corazón.[20]

It is such hyperbolic comparisons of a woman to the wonders of nature which later evolved into literary convention among the poets of the *dolce stil nuovo*. Yet the fact that stylistic conventions in Arab poetry strongly resemble the woman-worship and platonic love of the Provençal courtly tradition does not demonstrate influence of one on the other.

Bearing in mind both this similarity and that of the *kharjas* to Arab poetry of the same period, it is not surprising to find a resemblance between the *kharjas* and Provençal lyric as well. Not only does the invocation to physical love in many *kharjas* resemble that of the Provençal lyric, but the concentration on lovesickness, on suffering because of unrequited passion, is common to both. This similarity has been a prime argument on the one hand, for those who see Arab influence on Provençal lyric and popular peninsular lyric and on the other, for those affirming influence of Provençal lyric on the popular peninsular traditions. Each side has used the resemblances to prove its own case. Yet clear differences emerge between traditional peninsular lyric and Provençal lyric portrayals of woman.

While in the case of the *kharjas*, woman is totally subordinate to and dependent on man, in Provençal courtly love lyric and in the *cantigas de amor* she is practically a divine being with man her servant. And while the *kharjas* concentrate on the *lovesick woman* who longs for man for companionship and gratification and not as a means to ennoble herself, the Provençal tradition centers on the *lovesick man* who worships his lady, whose happiness is completely in the control of her whims, and who eventually spiritualizes her to the exclusion of all hope of physical gratification. Nor is woman portrayed as a goddess or viewed as an ennobling creature or a divinity in northern peninsular lyric. Furthermore, neither in the *kharjas* nor in northern peninsular traditional lyric is woman pictured as distant or placed on a pedestal by her lover; if anything the reverse situation is often the case, for frequently it is the man who is unreachable. Thus judging by their portrayals of woman it seems improbable that the *kharjas* were created through direct influence from the Provençal lyric. It is more likely that travelers or crusaders in Spain might have appropriated the themes of short traditional lyrics such as the *kharjas* or of sensual Arabic poetry heard on their travels; these frequently recited lyrics may then have developed more complex styles and thematic conventions on reaching Provence. Our next chapter will discuss further the possible influences on Provençal courtly love lyric.

It therefore appears doubtful that the portrayal of woman in traditional peninsular lyric differs from that in the epic because of the effect of European learned lyric. On the other hand critics such as Theodor Frings and Leo Spitzer believe the two types of lyric had a common origin in the so-called "Spring-song" in which woman played a major role. Basing his analysis on earlier research by Frings, Spitzer finds a similarity in content among the *kharjas* and *cantigas de amigo,* the *Frauenlieder* (German folk lyrics of the same period), and lyrics found to exist in many pre-Christian cultures including those of ancient Egypt, China, Greece, Scandinavia, Serbia, and Russia.[21] He suggests that spring has always encouraged young women "to throw off . . . the yoke of custom and law, the yoke of mothers and husbands, and to engage in gay, licentious celebration," and that a "pre-Christian framework of collective, improvised dancing songs of women in Springtime" existed in many cultures as an expression of this feeling.[22] The existence in numerous cultures of a lyric tradition in which woman appears passionately eager for male company would point to a spontaneous origin of this portrayal in the *kharjas* and *cantigas de amigo* on the basis of an innate human emotion. Yet Spitzer does not deal in detail with Castilian lyric and neglects to mention or explain the differences in the sensuality of female portrayals among the three regional lyrics of the peninsula. Thus if one accepts his theory of the origins of these lyrics and their portrayal of woman, then to explain why gradations of sensuality exist, one would have to assume that the differing values with respect to female morality and the differing views of woman's role in each of the three societies placed their imprint on the popular interpretation of a lyric theme common to many peoples.

Of all possibilities Spitzer's theory and the possible influence of Arabic society and mores seem the most rational explanations of the contrast between the popular lyric portrayal of woman and that of the epic tradition; but even if the spontaneous "spring-song," common to so many cultures, is the true origin of peninsular lyric in each region, and if Arab attitudes had no effect in causing the lyric of the north to depict the passionate nature of woman more than did the epic, the existence side by side of Arab and Christian cultures clearly explains to a large extent the divergences found between the peninsular lyric of the north and of the south. The disparity can be traced to our earlier discoveries concerning the differences in the position and role of woman between Moslem and Christian Spain of the early Middle Ages. We will recall that in Moslem Spain woman was considered an object for male sensual pleasure, whether as a wife or a slave. She spent her time indoors, caring for the home and pampering her body with oils and unguents to make herself more appealing to man. Monogamy was rare, and the family was not a close-knit group where members protected one another but rather a harem over which man ruled like a monarch. In contrast, life for northern woman was harsher and demanded more than her mere presence for man's benefit. The epic revealed the strength and unity of the family group, the pride of men in upholding woman's honor and their own, the ideal of monogamous marriage in northern Spain. Though marriages were often arranged, it was clear in such epics as the *Poema de Mío Cid* and the *Poema de Fernán González* that the possibility existed of a marriage for love in which respect and affection were as important as physical and economic concerns. This was certainly not the case in the south, judging by the historians. Furthermore, though women of northern Spain were certainly restricted and held in an inferior legal position, they did enjoy freedom and a better juridical position than in the south. The epics clearly show that in the north though men were dominant in the end, women did have their say and were accorded attention. In several of the epics, women were in fact the holders and wielders of power.

Clearly these differences in the two societies are reflected in the dichotomies we have noted in our examination of peninsular lyric. The more restrained eroticism of the northern lyric and the references to married love and motherly concern for and influence upon a daughter's behavior seem to reflect the moral system of northern Spain as observed in the epics, chronicles, and ballads. On the other hand, the *kharjas* mirror a society in which woman was revered as a love object at the beck and call of man rather than as loyal love, wife, mother, and center of the home.

Chapter Five

Women in Learned Lyric Poetry: Stereotype & Invention

In the third chapter of our study we attributed the change in the portrayal of woman from the Spanish epic to the ballads in part to a transformation in society during the period of the twelfth to fourteenth centuries. Though the nobility throughout Europe was struggling to control the power of the monarchs, the diminished emphasis on feudal wars had by this period turned the attention of people to more domestic, nonmilitary interests and to a cultivation of elegance in which woman could participate. The principal changes in this epoch were of a socioeconomic nature. The lessening threat of war encouraged the growth of large towns which soon became centers of commerce, while the growth of trade created a middle class which could afford to indulge itself with the purchase of luxury items. By displaying such possessions this middle class could attempt to increase its social prestige. The crusaders, who had opened new trade routes to the East, admired the beauty of the mozaics, fine cloth, luxurious carpets, and gardens and fountains of the Orient; they were not to deprive their homelands of the same elegance.[1] Hence the twelfth and thirteenth centuries introduced to the continent fine objects of art and elegant fabrics. Ornate clothes for both men and women became the fashion in the second half of the thirteenth century.[2] It is clear that the stage was set for the refinement of life in Europe.

We have already noted the probability that woman's importance increased in this newly emerging society of the late Middle Ages, judging in part by the greater prominence of feminine interests in the ballads as compared to the epics. The change in attitude toward woman in Spain is further reflected in a broadening of the legal rights granted to her by thirteenth-century society. We noted earlier the liberalizing trend in woman's juridical status as seen in Alfonso el Sabio's *Siete Partidas*. In comparison to such earlier codes as the *Fuero Juzgo,* Alfonso's laws reveal respect for woman and an expectation that men will treat her as a lady. His sympathy for women as human beings entitled to just treatment under the law is typified in Partida 4, Título 4, Ley 5, which declares that a woman must not be victimized by a man who promises to marry her unless he finds a richer or more honorable spouse in the meantime. Furthermore, the *Partidas* also contain laws providing for prosecution of rapists. The fact that Alfonso frowned on procuresses and prostitution substantiates our impression from other codes and the *Poema de Mío Cid* that the role most respected for woman was that of wife and mother, the center of the family group.

The *Partidas* also reveal a feminine ideal which will be mirrored in the poetry of the period. The ideal woman was of noble lineage and possessed beauty, good manners, and loyalty (2.6.1 and 2.7.11). Alfonso also felt that women of the court should be taught to read so that they might have "buen entendimiento" and be able to converse with men (2.7.11). The view that women should be trained in good manners and educated to provide intelligent conversation indicates an ideal of femininity which was certainly not emphasized in the epic, the ballads, or the popular lyric. We must look to the learned lyric for a portrayal of these new qualities.

Concomitant with the socioeconomic changes in late medieval Europe and the new interest in woman's femininity was the evolution of the cult of the Virgin. The veneration of Mary helped to dignify all women and slowly erased the moral stigma they had borne since Eve was said to have tempted Adam. Indeed one cannot separate the worship of the Virgin from the increasing regard for woman in the latter part of the Middle Ages. Even more difficult is the attempt to divide learned lyric veneration of woman in courtly love poetry from later lyric spiritualization of all women in the image of the Virgin Mary, for even the poetic idealization of woman as an object of physical love was related to the new regard for her which had in part grown out of the Marian cult.

Along with the new respect for woman, a change in her juridical status, and a general refinement of society came new developments in social mores, particularly in the relationship of men and women. It was a small, sophisticated segment of the population, the landed aristocracy of the south of France, which created an ideal of what woman should be and a complex system of behavior toward her. Their system of courtly love became so widespread that Johan Huizinga remarks: "In no other epoch did the ideal of civilization amalgamate to such a degree with that of love."[3]

"Courtoisie," or courtly love, included three basic and familiar tenets: elevation of the beloved to a position superior to man, the ennobling force for man of human love, and the necessity that desire remain unsatisfied. The yearning for possession could never reach physical fulfillment, for this would destroy the essence of the relationship, the desire itself. Ideally, then, man served and adored woman and sought her acquiescence in an emotional union. He did not conquer and dominate her.[4]

After the analysis in our previous chapters it is abundantly clear that this new attitude toward love placed women of the aristocracy in a much more favorable position than they had held in the past. This is especially evident when one discovers that women were the chief judges of lovers' complaints at so-called courts of love. One of the most well-known questions at the courts was whether love could exist between a husband and wife. The correct answer to this query was negative because proper courtly lovers grant each other everything but sexual favors without being coerced to do so, whereas marriage forces people to share whether they wish to or not.[5] Implied here is the fact that courtly love had to be an extramarital affair. Since many marriages were effected not out of choice but through convenient arrangement, that people should seek romance and intrigue elsewhere is a perfectly logical development.

An ingenious decision in a court of love conducted by Eleanor of Aquitaine concerned a woman who, despite her love for one man, had promised to grant her affections to her new suitor if ever she should lose the love of the first. Subsequently she married the man to whom she previously had granted her affections. Since an earlier court had declared marriage and love incompatible, the second lover demanded her affections as fulfillment of her promise. Although the lady refused, Eleanor, sitting in judgment, granted his request. Not only do these two examples reveal the technicality and *preciosité* of the strictly codified amenities involved in the art of courtly love, but they also indicate that love was treated almost as a commodity one could give or withdraw at will. Such an attitude would seem to imply that a courtly love relationship was a game to be played until one bored of one's partner rather than a serious emotional attachment.

The contents of Andreas Capellanus's *De Amore,* a work which instructed gentlemen in the art of love, supports these impressions. W. T. H. Jackson notes that Capellanus describes an art of persuasion for physical ends; woman normally accepts the statements of her suitor but is well aware of the insincerity with which they are offered.[6] Bearing in mind the questionable candor of many who practiced the courtly art, one is led to wonder about the sincerity of the learned lyric. Although a judgment on this must await further analysis, one cannot help suspecting that the adoration of women expressed by many troubadour poets was often just as transitory as the convention itself. It is equally doubtful that in all such relationships the ideal of unsatisfied desire was maintained in practice.

Recently Peter Dronke has proposed new ideas about courtly love which not only contradict most theories about its origins in lyric poetry but also suggest that its essence is not precisely as we have described it on the basis of generally accepted literary history.[7] Dronke does not support the idea that courtly love closely followed the model of a feudal relationship of service between man and woman. On the contrary, he feels that women were not served reverently by men but rather were loved at that time quite as they are today, and that only the "forms of poetic expression" were different.[8] Dronke sees no evidence in the lyrics to suggest that courtly love remained platonic. Though physical possession is not mentioned, this can be explained, he feels, by the fact that these were poems meant for public recital in a society with pretensions of refinement; the lyric went only as far as decency permitted. Dronke also denies the adulterous nature of courtly love; he points out that women involved in such a relationship were not necessarily married, citing the example of the heroine in the first part of the *Roman de la Rose.* He contends that the secrecy necessary in courtly love originated not from its adulterous nature but "rather from the universal notion of love as a mystery not to be profaned by the outside world; not to be shared by any but lover and beloved."[9] Dronke's position is based on his assertion that courtly love did not evolve as a new feeling and a new system in the eleventh century but that it is rather a view of love common to many peoples. His evidence for such a belief is discussed below.

The origins of the courtly love lyric are bound up in the obscure beginnings of the courtly love system itself. Early theories of liturgical origins or the influence of poetic attitudes found in classical Latin lyric have given way to other hypotheses such as the influence of Arabic poetry, the so-called "Spring-song" (which Spitzer and Frings believe to be the origin of the courtly love view of woman as well as of the popular lyric view) and Peter Dronke's belief that courtly love lyric is not unique in its view of woman.[10] In attempting to prove his own theory Dronke finds a similar view of love reflected in the earliest *popular* verse of Europe, citing examples from the oral lyric tradition of southern Spain (the *kharjas*), France, and Byzantium, as well as from more literary poetry dating from the Egypt of ca. 1160 B.C. and the Caucasus region of the twelfth century A.D. In these lyrics Dronke points out the worship of woman as divine incarnation, a source of strength and goodness, and a being to whom man willingly renders service. Often a guardian or confidant is present in these poems and there is also the possibility of male suffering caused by rejection. As Frings pointed out that characteristics of primitive popular European lyric can be found in even earlier poetry of distant regions, so Dronke shows that the characteristics of Provençal courtly love poetry can be found in both popular and learned lyric of earlier eras and far-away locations. Indeed, we ourselves found several courtly love themes in the traditional lyric of Castile (see chapter 4). Hence Dronke believes that Provence was not unique in contributing this particular view of love, but that its lyric enriched the means of expressing a common human emotion by evolving a more conceptual mode of expression through the influence of mystical, cosmological, philosophical, and theological language and ideas as applied to the beloved.

Though Dronke's arguments present a most attractive and convincing new point of view, attempts to seek conclusive proof must remain frustrated. The only certainty is that William IX was the first to incorporate the theories of courtly love into a poetry destined to be heard and read by knights and ladies of the courtly aristocracy during the feudal period. William sang of *amour chevaleresque*, that is, worship of and submission to a lady with explicit mention of physical fulfillment; but other poets of southern France soon expressed their love without the references to physical possession which were present in William's work.

Discussions in the courts of love are also reflected in the Provençal learned lyric. Huizinga mentions a particular poem which illustrates typical subject matter. The conclusion reached is that a man would prefer to hear his lady well spoken of and to find that she had misbehaved rather than to hear it rumored that she had not followed the codes of courtly conduct and to find that the rumors were false.[11] This type of reasoning again leads us to question the sincerity of the troubadour's own feelings, especially when the lyric seems to place such great importance on society's opinion and often relies on strictly conventional ways of expressing supposedly deeply felt emotions. This same problem has led one critic to remark that "when one of these troubadours actually did love his lady, he could scarcely find a mode of expression different from that established by the professional songsters. We are therefore continually balked when, lured by a note of apparently vibrant emotion, we try to guess whether behind the impassioned verse there lurks a genuine affection."[12]

Despite the Gallic influence brought to Spain through the eleventh-century Cluny movement and the pilgrimages to Compostela, the courtly troubadour lyric and its social graces were slow to take root in the central part of the peninsula. Sánchez-Albornoz attributes this to the cultural domination of the Arabs and the burden of constant wars which kept Spanish society at a rude and barbaric level, permitting Spain's nobility no leisure in which to develop the refinements which produced the new mores of courtly love.[13] The literary circles which were to parallel those creating the troubadour *cantigas de amor* in the thirteenth-century Portuguese court of Don Dionís did not reach their height in Spain until the fifteenth-century courts of D. Juan II of Castilla and Alfonso V of Aragón in Naples.[14] Of course some Provençal influence did filter into Spain much earlier, for even in the thirteenth-century court of Alfonso el Sabio there were many visiting poets from Provence and Cataluña who introduced the new literary trends.

In spite of the tardiness with which troubadour lyric arrived in Castile, its influences are found in certain works which preceded the fifteenth-century literary courts. The earliest example is an anonymous thirteenth-century lyric poem which clearly illustrates the incipient courtly treatment of woman in Spain. Although most critics agree that

the spirit of the *Razón feita de amor* is popular, no one can say that the
manner in which the poet describes his lady is typical of popular Spanish lyric poetry.

Indeed the very fact that the first characteristic mentioned of the
lady is her physical appearance indicates that her role in relation to the
poet is that of an object of physical love. A young man relaxing in a
fragrant meadow spies a young girl and proceeds to describe her from
head to toe in the conventionally prescribed troubadour manner. The
characteristics of her beauty also follow the patterns found in courtly
love poetry of the European tradition. The skin of her forehead is white,
her cheeks show shades of vermillion, her nose is straight, her mouth
and teeth well proportioned, and her lips full. Even if we were unaware
of her similarity to so many other troubadour ladies, we could certainly
see that this attention to description of feminine beauty is much more
thorough than anything we found in the popular lyric. The sensuality
of the description, greater here than in the popular lyric of the northern
peninsula though perhaps no greater than in some *kharja* descriptions,
certainly is now much more complex. We have, however, omitted one
quality of the young lady. Her dark eyes are probably a uniquely
Castilian characteristic, for the European convention normally requires
either blue eyes or so-called *yeux vairs,* which seemed to change color
with the surroundings.

Nonetheless, another quality of the young girl in the *Razón de amor*
removes her further from ladies of the popular lyric into the sphere of
European tradition. Her hat, gloves, and clothes of silk give an impression of elegance which characterizes her as a woman of the nobility.
She has attained a certain level of refinement which separates her from
rustic or bourgeois ladies. Further illustrative of the influence of European lyric are the idyllic surroundings which the poet uses as a setting
for the encounter. The troubadours of Provence often placed the action
of their songs in beautiful countryside, and the anonymous author of
Razón de amor has followed suit:

> Todas yerbas que bien olién
> la fuent cerca sí las tenié:
> í es la savia, í son as rosas,
> í el lirio e las violas
> . . . .

mas ell olor que dí ixía
a omne muerto resucitaría.[15]
(p. 15)

The month is April, time of rebirth and rejuvenation, and the scene is a totally voluptuous one with delectable perfumes, lush flowers and greenery, the warmth of the sun, and a streaming fountain. Such an introduction is clearly meant to stimulate the senses for what is to follow.

What does follow has been the subject of much critical discussion. Obviously the attraction the young girl offers for the poet is a physical one. Yet it is unclear whether the poem implies physical union. Such an implication would, of course, go beyond the Provençal tradition, in which poetic love remained platonic. Yet there are indications that our poet does find physical gratification. First of all, when he and the young girl recognize each other as admirers, the girl's actions are described explicitly, as they might be in the *kharjas*:

Tolíós el manto de los hombros,
besóme la boca e por los ojos.
(p. 17)

She subsequently replies to the poet's question saying that now "Conozco meu amado" (p. 18). Whether the use of *conocer* can be taken in the biblical sense is not certain, but it is a distinct possibility. Such a possibility seems more likely when one considers the fact that the poet clearly notes the presence of a silver goblet of wine placed in an apple tree for him by the girl. An association of wine with passion could be intended here. Furthermore, if a second half of the poem was originally part of the main portion, as Leo Spitzer believes,[16] then its contents substantiates a sexual union in the first part. Here we find a symbolic debate between wine and water in which the two are finally mixed. If, as Spitzer maintains, the wine represents sexual experience and the water, platonic love, then when the two are blended sexual union is indicated. Hence we have the likelihood that, as in specifying dark eyes, the poet has again removed his work from the European courtly attitude toward woman—this time in implying physical satisfaction as well as emotional love.

However, by no means have we exhausted the elements of the *Razón de amor* showing influence of the European lyric view of woman. Early in the poem we find the following statement:

> Un escolar la rimó/que siempre duenas amó;
> más siempre hobo crianÃ§a/en Alemania y en Francia;
> moró mucho en Lombardía/pora aprender cortesía
>   (p. 4)

The implication here is that a man could not be a success at "courting" ladies without education in the courtly art. Subsequently, in describing her lover in the *cantiga* she sings, the girl reveals the importance she places on the new, refined manner in which men were to treat women in aristocratic circles: "sabe muito de trobar,/de leyer e de cantar" (p. 17). Further along she admires her lover's *bonas maneras*. Though the Spanish epics also portrayed the nobility, such expectations on the part of woman were not present, for the social changes which brought them on had not yet occurred. Neither were such expectations mentioned in the popular lyric.

Other aspects of the poem also imply the influence of courtly male-female rélationships. The poet refers to the *cinta* and *alfayas* given to his lady as gifts, a common troubadour practice. Furthermore, at the start of the dialogue we discover that the girl has had contact with her lover only through messengers: "mas non coÃ±ozco mi amado/pero dizem' un su mendajero" (p. 17). This is truly worship from afar as it is depicted in the ProvenÃ§al troubadour lyric. In the sense that the lovers to that point had not met nor seen each other ("mas s'io le vies' una vegada" [p. 16]), there is even a slight reminder of the *amour lointain* of Jaufre Rudel.

Hence woman in the *Razón de amor* is certainly not venerated as wife, mother, and childbearer. She has no occasion to assert herself in the defense of her honor or her city, as in other epics, for emphasis is now strictly on the love relationship. The new position she holds as a gallantly treated beloved is also different from her role in Castilian popular lyric in that the stress is on physical love while the poet's attitude toward her follows new poetic conventions. Portraying her as a type, the poet does not give her an individual personality such as she had in some of the ballads. Yet at the same time, despite the new influence of the European tradition in creating the portrayal of woman in the *Razón de amor* there are still elements which seem to be purely Hispanic in nature. Not only does the young girl have dark eyes but she sings a *cantiga de amigo,* a popular form unique to the Hispanic lyric. Hence even with the influence of new European currents, this anonymous poet maintains an aspect of the portrayal of woman characteristic of Hispanic tradition and absent from the troubadour poetry of Provence.

Another early example of Castilian learned lyric which shows the effect of new European attitudes in its treatment of woman is the debate between Elena and María, a Leonese poem which Menéndez Pidal dates from the last third of the thirteenth century.[17] Their dispute, centering on the question of whether a cleric or a knight is preferable as a lover, was a popular subject for medieval poems. Although this poem does not idealize woman or place her on a pedestal, it contains certain elements which show that Elena and María have been influenced by the new mores of the middle or upper classes to which they seem to belong. Their attitudes toward men, including the manners and treatment they expect, are revealed as each defends her own lover and criticizes the other's. Yet their lovers remain on just as symbolic a plane as the idealized damsels of courtly lyric, for no truly personal and individual qualities are delineated.

María strikes first by defending the qualities of the "cleric," a man of letters, not necessarily a priest, in early poetry.[18] Her tone is moralistic as she stresses the fact that her cleric doesn't gamble or waste money foolishly (lines 1-5). Neither does he concern himself about arms or battles, for: "mas val seso e mesura/que siempre andar en locura" (pp. 47-48). Implied here is the tendency for a knight to be spendthrift, foolish, and a bit chaotic in life-style.

Yet even as she defends the cleric's moral uprightness and stability, María reveals another aspect of her own personality; while she disdains the wastefulness of the knight and considers it immoral, she herself is not impervious to material pleasures. Indeed she apparently feels that a cleric is more likely to provide them:

> El bibe bien onrrado/e sin todo cuydado;
> ha comer e bever/e en buenos lechos jazer;

ha vestir e calçar/e bestias en que cavalgar,
vasallas e vasallos/mulas e cavallos;
ha dineros e panos/e otros averes tantos.

(35-45)

Clearly it is the relaxed, bourgeois life María wishes to lead; and she has
nothing but scorn for the knight, for she feels he cannot provide it. In
contrast to the easy life of the cleric, she emphasizes the knight's mea-
ger meals and perpetual discomfort:

El pan a rraçion/el vino sin sazon
. . . come poco/ . . .
commo tray poco vestido/siempre ha fambre e frio
come mal e jaze mal.

(53-59)

Such considerations as a desire for the comforts of the domestic life
show the influence of the new wealth of the middle classes. Rare was
the woman of the popular lyric who talked of material pleasures. Of
course this contrast is probably related to the class difference between
the women of the learned lyrics and those of the popular lyrics.

A certain mocking attitude toward María can be inferred from the
fact that she continues to stress the wealth of the cleric. Not only does
she emphasize his quantities of wine, wheat, silver, money, clothing,
and coals (174-80)—in short, the "vida de rico omne" which he leads
(188)—but she also places importance on the cleric's position in the
social hierarchy. She talks of the great respect shown to her man by all
the kings, counts, *ricos omnes,* and knights, for they kiss his hand in
reverence (265-75). In the same breath María is both moralistic and
materialistic. Criticizing the fact that the knight often must pawn all his
possessions because of his nasty gambling habit, she draws the conclusion that this leaves him no money to purchase goods such as clothes,
flour, and bacon for his lady (130-60). So while she objects to the
morals of the knight, María is unable to see her own materialism and
the emphasis she places on appearances.

Happily for the fate of her lover, Elena is able to respond to María in
kind. She praises the merits of the knight, a man of bravery and action
rather than words. Disdaining the leisurely, passive life of a cleric she
prefers the excitement of war and danger. Indeed we even begin to

suspect an antibourgeois, antimaterialistic attitude as Elena criticizes
the cleric for passing his days eating, sleeping, and spending money
(112-13). Such a critical attitude is further indicated when Elena
lambastes the cleric for sleeping with many women (114-15). We begin
to suspect that she has a more sincerely moral position than María when
she says a cleric cannot tell good from evil. She accuses the couple of
living off gifts: "Bevides commo mesquinos/de alemosna de vestros
vezinos" (207-8) and implies social disdain for the concubine of a
cleric:

> Si tu fueres misa escuchar/tras todos te has de estar,
> ca yo estaré en la delantera/et ofreçeré en la primera
> ami leverán por el manto e/tu yras tras todas arrastrando;
> ami levarán como condesa,/a ti dirán como monaguesa.
>
> (213-20)

Elena digs even deeper when she accuses the cleric of greedily retaining
charity funds meant for hospitals and poor people (361-64) and of taking pleasure in the grief of widows and widowers because he has hopes
of obtaining their money (382-84).

Yet Elena has a materialistic side, in spite of the values she expresses
in criticizing clerical immorality. If her views are not attuned so strongly
to the bourgeois existence as are María's, nonetheless they reveal a desire for the elegant goods, refined life, and emphasis on manners which
are part and parcel of the new social mores. To Elena, just as to courtly
ladies, the knight represents a certain romanticism. He sleeps in the
castles of many cities, denying his sword and shield to no one. At-
tended by squires and vassals, he is the perfect picture of the handsome
courtier: " ¡Dios, que bien semeja! /açores gritando/ cavallos reninchan-
do . . ." (90-92). Indeed, Elena ridicules the appearance of the cleric in
comparison:

> Mas val un beso de infançon
> que çinco de abadon,
> commo el tu barvirrapado
> que siempre anda en su capa encerrado,
> que la cabeça e la barva e el pescueço
> non semeja sinon escueso.
>
> (100-105)

Yet despite the romantic aspects, the knight's life is not without its material benefits; Elena does not neglect the fact that he is paid in horses, mules, gold, and silver. Neither does she conceal her interest in the expensive clothes he obtains for her:

> A mi tien onrrada,/vestida e calçada
> viste me de çendal/e de al que mas val.
> (95-98)

Elena's ideas about men conform closely to the courtly pattern and she seems less bourgeois in her tastes than does María. To Elena part of the knight's charm lies in the fact that he displays the manners of *courtoisie:* "alegre vien e cantando,/palabras de cortes fabrando" (93-94). The attitude of Elena, as of the young girl of the *Razón de amor* who stressed the gentleman's *bonas maneras* as a point of attraction, clearly reveals the magnetism of the conventions of courtly love.

In this second learned poem we have found once more that woman is portrayed not as mother or wife, as might have been expected in earlier genres, but rather as a young girl whose values have been influenced by a changing society. A new bourgeois materialism and a desire for comfort and security on the part of one of the characters is balanced by the desire for elegance, the refined life, and the romantic attentions of a knight with courtly manners on the part of the other. The excellent in-depth portrayal of feminine psychology and values creates a more extensive and varied portrayal of woman than we have found either in epic or in ballad.

We have already mentioned that Alfonso el Sabio's thirteenth century court, renowned for the many learned men it attracted in the fields of history and law, was also a Castilian center of literary and musical activity in its day, drawing to it such Provençal troubadours as Giraut Riquer and Peire Vidal, who brought with them the savor of courtly lyric. In addition, it is the theory of Amador de los Ríos that Alfonso had received his early education in Galicia, a region which was the goal of pilgrims from many regions, including Provence. Because of these probable contacts with troubadour poetry, it is not surprising that Alfonso's *cantigas* to the Virgin Mary reveal the influence of foreign lyric.[19]

What is most interesting for us about the *cantigas* is the fact that although they are religious in inspiration, in them Alfonso's attitude toward Mary is often that of a courtly lover worshiping a fair damsel. The fact that Alfonso portrays the Virgin in a courtly context is especially evident in his prologue. Of the three previously mentioned elements usually considered characteristic of courtly love, Alfonso's worship of Mary clearly contains two. Loving the Virgin is morally elevating:

> Querendo leixar ben et fazer mal;
> ca per esto o perde e per al non.
> (Prólogo, 1:2-3)[20]

In doing evil he will lose her love, so to maintain her devotion he is inspired to do good. Secondly, Alfonso sees the Virgin as a superior being, just as a troubadour would portray his beloved:

> Querrei-me leixar de trobar des i
> por outra dona; e cuid'a cobrar
> per esta quant'enas outras perdi.
> (Prólogo, 1:2)

He calls himself a poet in love:

> Esta dona que tenno por Sennor
> e de que quero seer trobador.
> (Cantiga 10, 1:33)

Further, he often speaks of serving the Virgin, his *sennor.* Though he is referring to prayer and loyalty of a religious nature, here is a clear parallel to the situation of the troubadour lover serving his beloved as vassal to lord. When Alfonso praises the virtues of Mary he follows another lyric convention:

> Ca o amor desta Sen[n]or é tal,
> que queno á siempre per i mais val;
> e poi-lo gaannad'á, non lle fal,
> sennon se é per sa grand ocajon.
> (Prólogo, 1:3)

> pois en bondade crece cada dia
> e en beldade, de que sse pagar

> . . . .
> . . . Deus foi juntar
> en ela *prez* et sen et *cortesia*
> et santidade, u mercee achar.
>   (Cantiga 180, 2:199)

> . . . Deus lle quis dar
> todas estas cousas por melloria,
> porque lle nunca ja achassen par,
>   (Cantiga 180, 2:199)

Constancy, goodness, beauty, valor, courtesy and mercy are all familiar as qualities revered in woman of courtly lyric.

Alfonso also ascribes to the Virgin qualities which, while perhaps characteristic of the damsels in troubadour lyric, are not so ideal. Like many a lady, courtly or otherwise, the Virgin shows herself to be jealous, demanding loyalty of those who consecrate themselves to her service. The diatribe she directs at a previously devoted gentleman who has married shows Alfonso's very realistic portrayal of a jilted woman:

> Non es tu o que dizias
> qui mi mais que al amavas,
> et que me noytes e dias
> mui de grado saudavas?
> Por qué outra fillar yas
> amiga et desdennavas
> a mi, que amor ti avia?
> . . . .
> di, e porqué me mentiste?
> Preçaste mais los seus bees
> ca os meus? . . .
>   (Cantiga 132, 2:90)

While the *Milagros* of Berceo were written not for the erudite or the aristocracy but for the common people to hear, the descriptions of the relationships between the Virgin and the characters in some of his miracles bear a resemblance to some of Alfonso's portrayals. This parallel occurs particularly in the idea of service to the beloved and thus is related to the courtly tradition. In "La Casulla de San Ildefonso" we have the following description:

Sienpre con la Gloriosa ovo su atenencia,
Nunqua varon en duenna metió maior querencia,
En buscarli servicio methie toda femencia.[21]

Berceo describes the saint's major occupation in life as rendering services to the Virgin; and since he refers to Ildefonso as *el amigo leal,* she can be considered his lady. On the other hand, both poets depart from convention as they ascribe to Mary qualities of the ideal, though not necessarily courtly, woman. In both of their works the Virgin is kind, forgiving, sincere, moral, and motherly in caring for those devoted to her and in need of her aid. She is far more sympathetic to man's request for her affections than the fickle, hard-hearted courtly idol:

> Que non poderei en seu ben falir
> de o aver, ca nunca y faliu
> quen llo soube con merçee pedir,
> ca tal rogo sempr' ela ben oyu.
> (Prólogo, 1.3)

The fact that Alfonso seeks no lyric heights in his physical description of the Virgin also sets his work apart from that of the troubadours; in a religious context it would be inappropriate to apply the third element of courtly love, physical desire. Hence Mary is not portrayed with the emphasis on physical appearance so institutional in troubadour lyric. Another element which prevents complete identification of his Virgin with courtly ladies is the fact that the miracles she performs often present her on a human plane much more typical of Berceo's Virgin than of troubadour lyric ladies. When we read of how she "livrou a abadessa prenne" (Cantiga 7) and saved from drowning a monk on the way to see his *druda* (11), we must view her as no longer strictly a symbolic idealization of the perfect woman but rather as one who accepts the basic inconsistencies and flaws in human nature.[22] Hence Alfonso's portrayal of the Virgin combines both the conventions of a new lyric attitude toward woman and a more realistic, down to earth portrayal of the Virgin as motherly, sympathetic, and not above the realities of human conduct.

For full appreciation of the unique aspects of the *cánticas de serrana* in the *Libro de Buen Amor* of Juan Ruiz a brief summary of the origins and characteristics of the *pastourelle* or *pastorela* is essential. One type representing this genre originated in medieval Gaul.[23] At the height of its popularity from the end of the twelfth to the end of the thirteenth century, the northern French *pastourelle* was basically aristocratic in spirit, tinged with disdain for the lower classes and with a tone of caricature. In these poems the knight had the upper hand, for to him the encounter with a shepherdess was merely a means to obtain brief sensual pleasure, while she was ridiculed for her gullibility.[24] Hence if the well-known troubadour love song represented an idealization of the lady of the court, the northern French *pastourelle* can be considered a mockery of the rustic woman.

The *pastorelas* of Provence differ somewhat in tone, for as Edgar Piguet points out, they view the shepherdess in a spirit of equality rather than disdain, and the dialogue is basically a clever, sophisticated game in which the knight attempts many psychological ploys and the shepherdess responds in kind.[25] Though the encounters are scabrous, most *pastorelas* of Provençal composition do not include gross language, quite in contrast to the *cánticas de serrana* by Juan Ruiz.

Judging by the *pastorelas* of Marcabru and Bornelh it is clear that the shepherdess is given an important and fairly sympathetic role. In one poem recounted in the first person by Marcabru (p. 40),[26] the poet encounters a gay, carefree young girl who responds to his overtures by telling him that she is not chilly and does not need his help or protection: "Pauc m'o pretz si. 1 vens m'erissa,/Qu'alegreta sui e sana." Indeed her resistance is so firm that he is forced to plead: "Si m fossetz un pauc humana." ("If only you were a little bit more human to me.") Marcabru tries to flatter the *pastora* by insisting that her beauty is proof of her aristocratic background, while she insists on her humble lineage. There is no tone of disparagement or caricature and the girl never does succumb. Indeed the shepherdess matches the poet argument for argument until she wins and he departs, no doubt for greener "pastoras."

Furthermore in a *pastorela* by Giraut de Bornelh (p. 351) the shepherdess speaks with respect and refinement in offering friendship to a knight whose lady has just deceived him, but she makes it clear at the start that she intends to marry a man of her own social class, indicating that she is not one to be taken in. Clearly she is in command of the situation.

If the tone of the Provençal *pastorela* is idealistic and that of the French *pastourelle* saturated with disdain and caricature, the tenor of the four *cánticas de serrana* in the *Libro de buen amor* is realistic, leaning toward ridicule and burlesque. But what is the poet mocking and what were the origins of his point of view? Menéndez Pidal contended in 1919 that Juan Ruiz modeled his portrayals on a supposedly popular peninsular *serranilla* type based on the experiences of real women, not necessarily shepherd girls but more often rough, crude girls who guarded mountain passes in Spain.[27] He cited the Sintra fragment (of Sintra, Portugal) found in the *Cancionero de la Vaticana* (song 410) as an example:

> Na terra de Cintra
> a par d'esta serra,
> vi ua serrana
> que braadava guerra.[28]

Surely this shepherdess is not refined like the Provençal type and not gullible like the northern French lyric maidens but rather an aggressive and gruff woman who would jump out of the woods and demand the attention of a passing man, frightening him ("que braadava guerra"). For this reason Menéndez Pidal called her the *serrana guerrera* or *salteadora* type.

Pierre Le Gentil has vigorously opposed Menéndez Pidal's assertion that the fragment represents an ancient type of peninsular origin, pointing out that the theme of a man searching for aid in an attempt to navigate a mountain pass is a primitive one and not specifically Hispanic. He has found the same theme in the French *pastourelle:* "Bêle pastoure car m'enseigne/vers la cité le droit sentier."[29] Yet Le Gentil neglects the possibility that such a theme in French lyric could have received influence from a peninsular tradition. Neither does he prove his contention that the Sintra fragment could represent a lyric genre which existed in the repertoire of courtly love poets but was neglected by them for a long time. The French critic further suggests that the fragment might represent a type of lyric close to the *cantigas de escarnio* and *maldecir* which parody courtly genres in the Portuguese *cancioneiros.* Yet in essence the Sintra fragment and the *cantigas* mentioned are not very similar, and Le Gentil gives no examples of the aggressive, uncouth mountain girl in any early lyric outside the peninsula.

Both Menéndez Pidal and Le Gentil, no doubt, had their own reasons
for supporting or denying the existence of a peninsular pastoral tradition upon which Juan Ruiz may or may not have based his *cánticas de
serrana*. Ironically Luciana Stegagno Picchio has recently proven that
both critics were mistaken.[30] By reconsidering the entire poem in
which the Sintra fragment is found, our critic has shown that it was
composed subsequent to *El libro de buen amor* and thus could have
exerted no influence whatsoever on our poet.[31] She cleverly proves her
case by showing that the author of the poem is identifiable as a fifteenth-century courtesan and that the meter is *arte mayor*, in vogue in
the fifteenth century and courtly in nature. She further shows that the
genre of the poem, the *pregunta*, did not exist in primitive Gallego-
portugués lyric but rather is courtly in nature and first appears in *El
Cancionero de Baena*. It is typical of dialogue poetry composed for
courtly amusement. Even the rhyme scheme of the poem is shown to
appear in Baena but not in early Gallego-portugués lyric. Thus some
clever detective work has shown that there is no known peninsular
serrana until Juan Ruiz and that it was probably his very *cánticas*
which inspired the composer of the Sintra piece.

Armed with the knowledge that the Arcipreste's compositions are
probably completely original in inspiration we can now proceed to
clarify his intentions through a comparison of the narrative and lyric
version of each pastoral incident. The first *cántica* is preceded by a
description in *Mester de Clerecía* (stanzas 950-58) dealing with an occasion when the poet was lost rather inelegantly on foot in the snow with
no food.[32] On spying a girl who is tending cows he asks who she is and
she responds aggressively:

> Yo só la Chata resia, que á los omes ata.
> Yo guardo el pasaje é el portadgo cojo;
>
> Al que pagar non quiere, priado le despojo:
> Págam' tu, synon verás como trillan rastrojo.
>   (952-53)

When the Arcipreste tries to get by this rustic maiden she insists that he
promise her gifts, and further warns: "Conséjote que t'abengas, ante
que te despoje" (956). Finally he assures her of some adornments, and,

having achieved her mission by threats, the husky girl then happily *carries* the poet through the mountain pass.

Though this *serrana* appears crude and unfeminine, the *cántica* dealing with the incident exaggerates these qualities and adds others of an equally unappealing nature. The *serrana* jumps out at the poet and he proceeds to record her unpleasant physical appearance: "Gaha, rroyn e heda" (961), that is to say, "Leprous, vile, and ugly," details not present in the narrated version. Not only does she threaten him unless he gives her presents, but she now throws her shepherd's hook at him, causing him to fall. If in the narrated incident she was aggressive, now she uses brute force to get her way. Furthermore, there is action in the *cántica* which did not appear in the narrative; after Ruiz promises her jewelry, the *serrana* now drags the poet home, stuffs him with rustic game and cheese, and then orders him to undress:

> Luchemos un rato,
> lyévate dende apriesa
> Desbuélvete d'aques'hato.
> (971)

Since the use of *luchar* in this sense refers to sexual relations, the traditional roles of knight and shepherdess in Gallic poems are reversed here, for the lady now does the propositioning.[33] Of course Ruiz is not without his last licks:

> Ov'á faser lo que quiso.
> ¡Creet que ffize'buen barato'!
> (971)

Thus the first *cántica* turns out to be an exaggeration of the poet's narrated encounter with a bold and demanding mountain girl. Not only does she increase her demands in the *cántica*, but she backs them up with force.

Pierre Le Gentil suggests a possible source for the personality of this *serrana*, mentioning that in the fourteenth and fifteenth centuries French poets such as Machaut, Froissart, and Deschamps wrote so-called "sottes chansons" in which the girls were monstrous, ugly, and capable of taking part in "disputes ordurières," that is ribald, filthy disputes. He notes that this type of song is also found in the earlier

Chansonnier d'Oxford and thus may have been a tradition in existence outside of Spain before the time of our poet.[34] If this theory is correct, Juan Ruiz may have availed himself of an existing model, adding his own touch by applying the model to a pastoral situation; yet since we cannot truly term his poem ribald or obscene, Le Gentil fails to prove that the Spanish poet was familiar with this precedent.

Proceeding to the second episode, the Arcipreste tells of becoming lost in the mountains and asking a *serrana* for the route. If she refuses, "Morarme hé convusco," he says (975). She promptly rejects him ("Sseméjasme sandío, que así te convidas") and threatens to do him physical harm if he approaches (976). As she carries out her threat the poet describes her actions:

> Dióme con la cayada tras la oreja fita,
> Derribóme cuest'ayuso é cay estordido;
> Ally prové que era mal golpe el del oyodo.
> (977-78)

As the Arcipreste lies bruised on the ground the bullying *serrana* gaily informs him that he should not take this joke seriously and invites him to her cabin proposing "que jugásemos al juego por mal del uno" (981), that is to say, another *lucha*. However, our poet demands a meal first, for "sy ante non comiese, non podría bien jugar" (982). The *serrana* does succeed in luring him to bed after the meal, though the poet merely states it is in payment for the *merienda*, quite in contrast to French and Provençal poets, who would assert that they would leap at such an opportunity. After satisfying her desires, our poet leaves the cabin as quickly as he can, muttering that the *serrana* has become angry and that he is frightened. In the Gallic poems a poet often found himself frustrated but never frightened.

The corresponding *cántica* concentrates on the episode in which the *serrana* hurls her staff at the poet, nearly knocking him unconscious, in an effort to show him she does not welcome his presence and his interest in her. This lyric version then jumps to a scene in which the *serrana* has taken the Arcipreste to her home for a meal. The payment she demands is the same as in the first song, but the poor poet cannot measure up to her needs this time, and her threats reveal another girl who does not hesitate to dominate a man, bending him to her will. Furiously she screams:

> Yo t'mostrare sino' ablanda,
> como se pella el eriso
> sin agua e syn rrocio.
>   (992)

That is to say, I'll show you how easily I can make you do as I wish.

As in the previous *cántica* this girl is a total brute. One doubts that the poet will be able to take his leave as safely and easily as in the narrative version. And in common with the first *cántica,* the second is also shorter than its narrative version and focuses on the mountain girl's lack of conventional femininity and her extremely domineering attitudes, showing us no amorous involvement on the part of the poet.

Thus in his second encounter with a *serrana* we again find a situation quite different from both the *pastourelle* and the *pastorela.* In contrast to the northern French poets' efforts, our poet's attempt at persuasion and seduction is short-lived. No gullibility on the part of the girl is evident. In contrast to the usual pattern of the southern French poems, after one brief attempt at flattery our poet reveals not the slightest affection or interest (who can blame him?), and again we find it is the girl who takes an aggressive role in the adventure and it is she who does the propositioning.

The *serrana* of the next episode is a more naive type, somewhat reminiscent of the gullible shepherdesses typical of northern French *pastourelles.* In the narrative Juan Ruiz comes across a shepherdess who mistakes him for a shepherd and imagines he wishes to marry her:

> Cuydós' cassar comigo como con su vesino
> Preguntóme muchas cosas: cuydós' que era pastor.
>   (993)

The poet does nothing to rectify her miscalculations, and we have the impression that she is simple-minded and easy to deceive. Although the narrative is very brief, in his *cántica* the poet elaborates on his adventure and makes the *serrana* appear even more foolish. As he approaches her the Arcipreste states outright that he is seeking to marry. Immediately, then, it is clear that he is planning to mock the girl. She, in turn, tries to entice him by enumerating her charms. The poets of the troubadour *pastorelas* praised the physical charms of the shepherdesses, much to their annoyance; but our young lady describes her rustic abilities, talents more reminiscent of a stable boy than of an attractive maiden:

> Bien sé guardar mata
> É yegua'n çerro cavalgo
> Sé'l lobo como se mata:
> Quando yo en pos dél salgo,
> Ante l'alcanço qu'el galgo.
>   (999)

She is somehow under the delusion that killing wolves, taming bulls, feeding cows, and riding bucking broncos are qualities which increase her appeal. What is more ridiculous is that Juan Ruiz pretends to agree to marry her, for it is clear that he would never commit himself to such a fate. Thus he succeeds in making mock of the gullible *serrana,* who takes him quite seriously and proceeds to list the wedding gifts she expects him to lavish upon her.

In each *cántica,* then, the Arcipreste creates a comic exaggeration of his narrated encounter. If in the supposedly real episode the mountain girl is crude and threatening, she becomes brutal and gross in the lyric version. If she appears naive in the encounter, her innocence is ridiculed in the lyric version, for in trying to make herself seem more attractive she chooses the very elements which would be least likely to inspire a mate of the poet's caliber. Yet why does Ruiz exaggerate the negative qualities of the girls? The Provençal tradition idealized rustic realities, describing the shepherdesses as feminine, delicate, and appealing. Our poet seems to do just the opposite; instead of idealizing a narrated incident in his lyric, he emphasizes the worst and least feminine aspects of the shepherdesses.

The Arcipreste's treatment of the final *serrana* provides a solution to this dilemma. In the narrative he meets a mountain girl more hideous than any up to now. This girl is truly an ugly monster, and the poet describes her in full detail. He notes her "espantable vista" (1011), her "dyentes anchos é luengos, cavallunos, maxmordos" (1014), and then says that she had "la cabeça mucho grande syn guisa;/cabellos chicos, negros, como corneja lysa;/ojos fondos é bermejos; poco é mal devisa" (1012). At times the poet's description actually reaches animalistic proportions:

> Las orejas tamañas como d'añal borrico;
> El su pescueço negro, ancho, velloso, chico.
>   (1013)

A year-old burro must have rather large ears indeed. In addition, hers is clearly not the long, graceful neck of a swan. The description proceeds gradually from head to toe, each detail more grotesque than the last, and many too vulgar to enumerate here. The fact that her smallest finger was larger than the poet's thumb and her wrist wider than his entire hand is almost a compliment to contrast to other details he mentions. This creature is a complete horror and certainly enough to frighten anyone coming upon her in a lonely mountain pass. Clearly she is not a model of courtly or even rustic beauty. Anthony Zahareas points out that the Arcipreste creates a ludicrous distortion of the courtly rhetorical portrait codified in the medieval "artes poéticos."[35] Juan Ruiz takes every aspect of the medieval ideal of feminine beauty and changes it to the monstrous. The use of such a burlesque from head to toe proves that the poet must have been aware of the troubadour ideals of beauty, ideals present in *pastorelas* as well as in courtly love lyric.

However, when we come to the *cántica* version of his encounter, we meet a very lovely young lady. Her appearance meets that of the ideal shepherd girls of tradition: "Fermosa, loçana/e byen colorada" (1024). For the first time in the *cánticas*, we really cannot question the femininity of this Juan Ruiz shepherdess, for the girl neither threatens the poet nor uses physical force against him. She keeps her voice down and seems quite demure; her inclinations are certainly maidenly, for she shows an interest in receiving gifts of clothing, itemizing an extensive list of requests: "una çinta," "buena camisa" (1035), "buena toca," "çapatas" (1037). The poet claims he is willing to grant her these things in payment for her hospitality but says that he will have to return with them later. Not trusting him, she rejects the poet's offers—an outcome quite common in the Provençal *pastorela*. Thus this *cántica* closely resembles the typical southern French lyric in which an attractive rustic maid disputes with a knight and finally turns him away. Yet it is significant that this is the lyric version of an encounter with a hideous girl. After three previous *cánticas* which exaggerated reality in the direction of the grotesque, the fourth idealizes a horrendous reality. The poet has performed a total about-face, a feat not infrequent throughout his book.

Yet how are we to interpret his turnabout? In the fourth episode our poet first shows how a peasant girl can appear in reality as he brings out the worst possible characteristics in his narrative. This is followed immediately by an idealization in the *cántica*, for the shepherdess here bears no resemblance to the one the poet described at first. Surely there must be an ulterior purpose to this about-face. It seems reasonable to suggest that our poet intended his fourth song as an ingenious burlesque of the artificiality of the Provençal portrayal of peasant girls and a mockery of the implicit blindness of this genre to true rustic conditions. The groundwork for such a parody is laid by the first three *cánticas*. Their setting in frigid mountain passes rather than in blossoming meadows; their emphasis on money, material objects, and food rather than on beauty and the finer senses; their exaggeration for the purpose of creating such frightening, boorish girls—all this makes the final idealization of deformity totally ridiculous.[36] Thus the tone of the *cánticas* blends superbly with the generally satiric nature of the Arcipreste's whole book.

The learned lyric concerned with the worship of woman exerted strong influence upon the late fourteenth- and early fifteenth-century works of the Marqués de Santillana. In some of his lyrics woman is portrayed not only in the courtly tradition of the Provençal and Galaico-Portuguese troubadours but also with a new perspective adopted in Spain by Santillana from the latest trends in Italian lyric of the fourteenth century. In still other lyrics woman appears not at all as the refined, elegant lady of the courtly mold.

It is important to bear in mind the changes which occurred in Italian learned lyric during the fourteenth century. While Italian poets developed the Provençal poetic attitude toward woman into spiritualization and deification of the beloved, in the next generation Petrarch moved towards a more realistic portrayal of woman in lyric poetry. His Laura is not an abstraction or a divine symbol (although she was increasingly idealized, especially after her death), but rather a woman of beauty with personal appeal.[37] A further development of importance for us is the growing trend toward erudition. On the threshold of the Renaissance, Italian poetry of the fourteenth century reveals the new interest in classical antiquity through its latinizing and puristic language, numerous references to mythology, and, particularly in the case of Dante, through a growing use of allegory based on classical sources. The fact that the Marqués de Santillana was influenced by these new developments is clear in what Gracía de Diego calls his latinizing mania, in his mannered style, and in the profusion of his references to mythology and tales of heroism.[38] Most important, we will also find it evident in his treatment of woman.

As we noted previously, much of the Marqués's lyric does reveal the influence of the Provençal troubadour lyric view of woman. In his "Loor de la Reina María de Aragón" he praises the queen's qualities in terms of courtly lyric description of feminine virtues: *honestat, buen, fablar, claridat, angélico viso* (García de Diego, pp. 177-80). The many *cantigas* and *dezires* he dedicated to young ladies also contain these conventions of courtly lady worship, as is evident in this *dezir:*

> Aurora de gentil mayo
> puerto de la mi salud,
> perfección de la virtud
> e sol candor e rayo . . .
> . . . .
> ¿Quién vió tal feroçidat
> en angélica figura
> Nin en tanta fermosura
> indómita crueldat?
> (García de Diego, pp. 192-93)

Here we find the familiar comparison of the lady's charms to the beauties of nature, the usual superlatives to describe her appearance and references to the perfection of her virtue and to her disdain of his courtship. A *canción* shows the conventional suffering of the lover:

> Recuerdate [a la dama] que padesco
> e padesçi
> las penas que non meresco
> desque ví
> la respuesta non devida
> que me diste.
> (García de Diego, p. 223)

However, totally new and distinct from this characteristic troubadour treatment of woman are such poems as the "Planto de Pantasilea" (pp. 135-45) in which a woman of antiquity, the queen of the Amazons, is viewed as a tragic heroine because of her ill-fated love for Hector, the Trojan hero. Here we no longer have courtly woman-worship but rather an episode of classical antiquity far removed in time and place. Classical antiquity in the form of mythology also appears in Marqués's "Loor a la Reina María de Aragón," mentioned above; in addition to the obviously courtly veneration of the queen's "perfecta belleça" she is compared to a Roman goddess: "Con voluntat muy sincera/Venus vos fiço heredera." Whereas the troubadours had portrayed the woman of their day as a symbolic idealization, the early Renaissance style now removes her further from reality by comparing her to the mythological figures of a former time.

The *Sonetos fechos al itálico modo* indicate Santillana's new bent by their very title. Though many of the sonnets have moral, religious, and political themes, a number do deal with love, and in so doing they combine the influence of the courtly ideal of feminine beauty and male suffering, the *dolce stil nuovo* spiritualization of the beloved, and early Renaissance references to classical mythology. The descriptions of the beloved, revealing her to be one of the sophisticated, "beautiful people" of her time, are sensual but with no implication of carnal love:

> Non es el rayo de Febo luçiente
> Nin los filos d'Arabia mas fermosos
> Que los vuestros cabellos luminosos.[39]

Though the inclusion of these conventions is not surprising given the fact that the poet may be playing the game of courtly love and perhaps be describing a nonexistent lady, even in poetry which he dedicates to women presumably closer to his heart the troubadour ideals are still to be found in profusion. Indeed, María Rosa Lida's indication that the "Cantar a sus fijas" follows the "canon medieval de belleza femenina" is clearly correct in the Marqués's description of his daughters:

> Fruentes claras e luzientes
> las çejas en arco alçadas,
> las narizes afiladas,
> chica boca e blancos dientes,
> ojos prietos e rientes.
> (García de Diego, p. 266)[40]

This description parallels that of the Arcipreste's fourth narrated encounter, without, of course, the gross exaggeration of details. Hence we have further reason to believe Juan Ruiz was mocking the rhetorical portrait. Note again in Santillana's poem the dark eyes, found also in the *Razón de amor* and probably the one uniquely Hispanic character- istic in the portrait of these girls. Further description of his *fijas* is very sensual; consider the following portrait:

> Carnoso blanco e liso
> cada qual en los sus pechos,
> porque Dios todos sus fechos
> dexó quando fer las quiso,
> dos pumas de paraiso
> las sus tetas ygualadas,
> en la su çinta delgadas
> con aseo adonado.
> (García de Diego, p. 266)

Though Santillana presumes to discover these voluptuous young ladies as *serranas* in the mountain foothills, we see through this guise as his description of their clothing reveals them to be aristocrats:

> Ropas trahen a sus guisas
> todas fendidas por rrayas,
> do les paresçen sus sayas
> forradas en peñas guisas
> suso ropas bien asentadas,
> de filo de oro brocado.
> (García de Diego, p. 268)

There is a certain coldness and distance between the poet and the ladies described both in Santillana's courtly lyric and in his poems in- spired by the Renaissance. Indeed almost every critic who touches on these poems agrees that he seems to feel no sincere personal involve- ment. García de Diego (p. xxix) cites particularly the *sonetos* in noting that Santillana seems to have chosen the love and veneration of woman merely as a subject for pretty lyrics and a theme around which he can reveal his mythological virtuosity. Even in his lyrics to the Virgin there is no humanization, no involvement of the poet, as there was in the poetry of Alfonso X and even of Berceo. Santillana merely uses a series of trite metaphors to praise her glory, as in "Los Gozos de Nuestra Señora": "fontana de salvación," "flor de las flores," "nuestra claror" (pp. 147-54).

It is in his works of a more popular tone that Santillana's portrayal of woman is at its most sincere and original. In one *villancico* (García de Diego, pp. 261-63) the form of the poem and the intimacy with which the girls' feelings are expressed clearly do not belong either to the troubadour lyric tradition or to the new developments of the early Italian Renaissance. The theme is simple and sincere: our poet comes upon three young ladies in a rustic atmosphere who are singing of the suffering and yearning love has caused them. It is the girls' feelings which are stressed, not the troubadour's, and thus the essence of the poem is closer to popular peninsular lyric than to poetry of European learned influence. Though he calls them "gentiles damas," the fact that the girls express themselves in *villancicos* places them on a more popular level. In each traditional refrain a girl complains of love. One explains how closely she is watched at home, another says she cannot sleep alone, and the third hopes God will take vengeance on her presumably disloyal lover (*villano*). The poem is short and simple, the language direct. The fact that Santillana composed the poem around traditional refrains helps make the girls seem quite real to us. No long, descriptive, exaggerated passages destroy the intimacy of the scene. No courtly conventions disguise the expression of true feelings.

There is yet another type of lyric in which Santillana shows originality in portraying the opposite sex. He composed ten *serranillas,* quite varied in length, style, and depiction of woman, though they are all brief and lack the extensive dialogue of the northern and southern French *pastourelles.* Indeed, they are even shorter than the Arcipreste's *cánticas,* and so there is little time to develop a detailed personality for the shepherdess. In his first *serranilla* we find an aggressive woman who appears "sin argayo," implying that she is strong, sturdy, and not particularly feminine. Her assertiveness frightens the *caballero* a bit:

> ¡Ay que en ora buena venga
> aquel que para Sanct Payo
> desta yrá mi prisonero!
> E vino a mi, como rayo,
> diziendo: "Preso, montero."
> (Cortina, p. 135)

When our *serrana* discovers that this gentleman is not the man she was waiting to capture, she invites him to her home:

> Perdonad amigo:
> mas folgad ora conmigo,
> a dexad la montería.
> (Cortina, p. 136)

As was the case in the Arcipreste's *cánticas,* this girl shows neither reticence nor refinement but rather she takes the initiative, expressing her desires brusquely.

Other *serranillas* by Santillana confirm the resemblance to the creations of Juan Ruiz. In his fourth the shepherd girl is again aggressive and proposes a "fight":

> Convien en toda figura,
> sin ningund otro partido
> que me dedes la cintura,
> o entremos a braz partido
> ca dentro en esta espesura
> vos quiero luchar dos pares.
> (Cortina, p. 139)

Recalling that *luchar* refers to sexual fulfillment, we once again have a *serrana* who actually tries to force physical involvement. In this approach she seems almost a sister to the Arcipreste's *serrana* of his first *cántica* who also proposed a *lucha.* Santillana's description of the subsequent activities, though anything but refined, is not scabrous as were some of the northern French *pastourelles:*

> Como aquel que non sabía
> de luchar arte nin maña,
> con muy gran malenconía
> arméle tal guardamaña
> que cayó con su porfía
> cerca de unos tomellares.
> (Cortina, pp. 139-40)

Since the events of these two poems are so different from those in Provençal poems of similar theme and so similar to some of Ruiz's *cánticas* we must note the possibility that Santillana was influenced by the tone and parodic bent of the latter.

Yet if Santillana did have in mind the conventions of the *pastorela*

and of the *cánticas* of Juan Ruiz, his own interpretations add new elements. References to war against the Moors and to countryside dotted
with olive trees can only represent events and local color of Spain
(*Serranilla* 5) rather than external influence. Furthermore, the simple
rebuttal and lack of prolonged debate such as we find in *Serranilla* 6
seem unique to Santillana rather than part of a European tradition:

> Bien vengade,
> que ya bien entiendo
> lo que demandades:
> non es deseosa
> de amar, nin lo espera,
> aquessa vaquera
> de la Finojosa.
>   (Cortina, p. 143)

Thus in several respects Santillana is independent of European convention in his *serranillas*: his lyrics lack the sophistication and complexity of action and dialogue so typical of their European counterparts; his knights do not show the same disdain or ridicule of the
shepherdesses as those of the French *pastourelles,* and the girls are
more outspoken, demanding, and even vulgar in his lyric than those in
Provençal verse; there is little coarseness in the description of sex; and
in a case where the shepherdess refuses his advances, the lover simply
accepts rejection and does not proceed to persuade and cajole her to his
point of view. Santillana usually treats his *serranas* with respect, tenderness, sympathy, and gentleness, and the social class difference so evident in the French versions is not emphasized here.

Therefore one must question generalizations such as Guillermo Díaz
Plaja's statement that Santillana's *serranillas* are of the type proceeding
from Provence.[41] Certainly there is no denying the influence of Gallic
pastourelles. The sixth poem, for example, is not clearly placed in
Iberian geography but rather in an idealized pastoral setting typical of
Provençal and French reverence for the country life:

> En un verde prado
> de rosas e flores,
> guardando ganado,
> con otros pastores. . . .
>   (Cortina, p. 142)

The courtly influence is also seen in the fifth poem, for the poet spies a beautiful *serrana* (her beauty in itself a European convention) but remains loyal to his lady love:

> Si mi voluntad agena
> non fuera, en mejor logar,
> non me pudiera excusar
> de ser preso en su cadena.
> (Cortina, p. 140)

Also typical of the European genre is the poet's promise that he will do anything if the shepherdess accepts his proposition, even join her as a shepherd if she refuses to leave the hills. *Serranilla 9* shows that this type of cajoling works as successfully in Spain as in Provence:

> Asy concluymos
> el nuestro processo
> sin fazer excesso,
> e nos avenimos.
> E fueron las flores
> de cabe Espinama
> los encubridores.
> (Cortina, p. 145)

Yet our previous analysis has shown that Santillana's *serranas* are not all pure imitation and that several of his lyrics could be a conscious mockery of the conventional *pastorela*, possibly under the influence of the Arcipreste's parodic *cánticas*. Thus in uniting several views of the shepherdess Santillana has shown more originality in portraying woman than he did in his erudite lyric. The result is a series of shepherdesses who retain some of the refinement and delicacy of their Provençal counterparts while still maintaining a certain crudeness typical of the Hispanic tendency towards the realistic, but without the grossness of the *serranas* of Juan Ruiz.

The passage of numerous European pilgrims to Compostela spread the love songs of Provence to northwest Spain. In the court of Portugal this lyric soon inspired poetry in the Gallego-portugués language, poetry which reached its apogee in the court of Don Dionís (1279-1325) among such poets as Nuno Fernandez Torneol, João de Guilhade, João Zorro,

Martin Codax and King Dionís himself. Under the hegemony of their
cantigas de amor most troubadour poetry in Spain tended to be written
in the Gallego-portugués tongue, and it was not until about 1445 that
the first collection of troubadour lyric in the Castilian dialect was
made by Juan de Baena. The poems of the *Cancionero de Baena,*
representing fifty-four named and many anonymous poets, can be divided into several types depending on their sources of inspiration.[42] In
addition to mythological, allegorical, and didactic works reminiscent of
some of the erudite lyric of the Marqués de Santillana, the *Cancionero*
contains earlier lyric of courtly love inspiration, notably that composed by Villasandino (who wrote between 1370 and 1424) and other
poets of his generation. Since these poets were at their height at a period subsequent not only to the flowering of the courts of Provence but
also to Petrarch's lyric creation, it should not surprise us to find in
Cancionero lyric traces of the traditions of Provençal troubadour portrayal of woman and also of certain attitudes introduced by the Italian
poet. We have already noted that Petrarch's lyric reveals a more con-
tinuous and more personal involvement with one particular woman
than did the lyrics of any Provençal poet. His poetry is also character-
ized by detailed physical description as well as linguistic subtleties,
plays on words, and a variety of metaphors comparing the physical features of his lady to the beauties of nature. These new metaphors are
evident in the *Cancionero.*

The existence of any influence upon the poems of the *Cancionero*
from Spanish popular lyric is vigorously denied by Menéndez Pidal;
the learned philologist points out that any Castilian lyric revealing
such influence was purposely omitted by Baena in an effort to present a
picture of court and palace lyric only.[43] Hence though we found popular lyric influence on the poetry of Ruiz and Santillana and even in the
Razón de amor, this will presumably not be the case with the *Cancionero
de Baena.* Whether the resulting portrayal of woman in the *Cancionero*
is pure imitation of external currents or will contain a certain degree of
sincerity and originality remains to be seen.

The first indication of the lyric attitude toward woman which will
prevail in the *Cancionero* is found in Baena's prologue, where he gives
the following description of how a poet should behave towards her:
"Noble, hidalgo, y cortés y mesurado y gentil y gracioso y pulido y
donoso y que tenga miel y azúcar y sal y donaire en su razonar, y otrosí

que sea amador."[44] Clearly then, this ideal poet belongs to the new
aristocracy rather than to epic society, in which masculine vigor was the
ideal. Subsequent poems fit in well with this description of the refined
poet-courtier, for most of the poets who center their lyric on woman
portray her as one who would expect such manners in her lover. Innumerable are the lyrics which praise the beauty, coloring, grace of
movement, honesty, courtesy, and kindness of the particular women to
whom they are dedicated. Villasandino sums up several conventions of
the courtly lyric worship of women:

> Lynda, graçiossa, real,
> clauellina angelical,
> la joya que por señal
> atendi e non la he,
> pero seruiendo leal
> syenpre la atendere.[45]
> (1.50)

In other poems (such as 1.1 and 1.46) Villasandino again expresses his
reverence for the same physical and moral qualities. Similarly, in Imperial's words woman's qualities make her a goddess:

> Por la pressençia de la qual beldat,
> estrellas luçiferas, muy esforçadas
> peresçen su luz e su claridat,
> assy oscureçen e sson escripsadas;
> (2.238)

This exaggerated praise, clearly typical of the courtly love treatment of
woman, contains comparisons which remind us of the way Petrarch and,
later, Garcilaso described their loves in terms of cosmic phenomena.

The almost ritual submission to conventions does not stop here, for
Imperial describes a woman in extremely elegant dress, further proof
that the noblewoman's preoccupations had changed since the epic:

> De vn fino xamete gris,
> Traya vna opalanda,
> enforrada en çendal vis,
> de juncos vna guirlanda;
> (2.248)

He also praises her talents:

> ¡O tu poetría e gaya ciencia!
> ¡O desir rrymico engeniosso!
> ¡O tu rectorica e pulcra loquencia!
> ¡e ssuauidat en gestos graciosos!
>   (2.238)

In another of his poems (2.248) his lady reveals her virtuosity by speaking in French, indicating without question that respect for woman was no longer based on her family role or on defense of her honor but on her level of education and culture.

Numerous other poems, in many cases filled with comparisons of women to mythological heroines or goddesses of antiquity, follow the conventions of woman-worship begun by the troubadours. Woman's ennobling powers over man have already been mentioned as a *lieu commun* of courtly love lyric. It is found as well in Villasandino:

> Vuestra lindesa e beldat,
> fermosura e onestat
> me fase seguir bondat
> onrrosa,
> ssya auer ningunt pavor
>   (1.7 bis)

Certainly there is nothing unique or original in this type of praise nor in another lyric by the same poet indicating loyal service of the court gentleman to his lady: "Syempre sere en seu mandado . . . Como syruo omildosa," (1.17). A further troubadour convention is found in poems lamenting the suffering the poet must endure because he is a prisoner of his affection, although his lady has refused him: "Soy presso en vuestro poder"; "Vos me pusistes en prision/do eu non poss salyr," (Villasandino, 1.43; see also 1.7, 8, 27, 44). Other topics appear in lyrics which portray the poet as totally subordinate, inferior, and clinging to his lady's affections for mere existence. Pero Gonçales de Mendoça reveals his dependence in the following manner when his lady leaves to begin life in a convent:

> Pves del mundo es partida
> la vuestra muy grant nobleza,

. . . .
morire desanparado
con pessar e con tristesa.
(2.251)

Macias practically falls to his knees in humility and submission:

E non dexes tu seruiente
perder por olbidança
. . . .
Non por mi mereçimiento
que a ty lo manda;
mas por tu merçed complida
duelete del perdymiento
en que anda
en aventura mi vyda;
(2.307)

This extension of humility to the point where the poet deplores his own merits before his lady is also present in a poem by Imperial:

Senora, yo non meresco
atan grant onrra aver;
todavia me ofresco
presto al vuestro querer. . . .
(2.248)

Finally, just as in conventional troubadour lyric, woman of the *Cancionero de Baena* demands loyalty of her lover and distrusts man:

Escudero, conviene vos morir,
pues que por otra dexastes a my,
e yo vos fare que desde aqui
vos nunca seades para otra seruir.
(Anonymous, 2.241)

And:

Ca dis vn exenplo: Quien cree a varon
sus lagrimas syembra con mucha tristesa.
(Fernand Sanches Talavera, 3.538)

There is a certain coldness about woman in the *Cancionero*. Often she seems no more real, no more truly of flesh and blood than are her ancestors of the conventional troubadour lyric of the earliest days. The deeper personal feelings and variety of emotions of Petrarch do not seem to have made an inroad, for the cries and laments of these poets, expressed in such trite metaphors, fail to convince us of sincere passion and fail to portray women who provide any unique reasons for inspiring such a passion.

As we noted earlier, a common pastime in the Provençal courts was discussion and debate on some intricate problem involving manners of courtly behavior. The *Cancionero de Baena* contains such debate in the form of poetic exchanges. For example, Diego Martines de Medina poses the following question to Isabel Gonçales, "Manceba del Conde de Niebla" in a poem dedicated to her praise:

> Por ende, yo contemplando
> en vuestra grant perfeçion,
> vos propongo tal quistion
> e omilmente demando,
> sy algund omne amando
> syn ninguna esperança
> biue en mayor folgança
> que del todo lo dexando.
>   (2.329)

Probably the poet is referring to his own hopeless love. His lady's response is given in the *Cancionero* by a *fraile:*

> Todo loor absoluto
> a solo Dios pertenesçe,
> e lo al çierto paresçe
> disfamoso, disoluto
> que nunca puede ser junto
> en vn cuerpo
> perfeçion,
> saluto toda corrupçion
> pues en sy es tan corruto.
>   (2.330)

Clearly the context is religious, with the implication that courtly love worship of woman as perfection incarnate is actually blasphemous.

Another dialogue centers around a problem seemingly technical in nature. Juan Alfonso de Baena, the compiler of the collection, debates with Ferrand Manuel which is more important in courtship:

> Ver mi amiga e nunca fablalla
> o syenpre fablalla e nunca miralla.
> (3.369)

While one poet defends the position that conversing with a lady is the way to know her best, the other feels that hearing her does a lover no good if he does not know what she looks like. Fray Diego de Valençia responds as the judge:

> E por que la vysta es causa notoria
> para ver a Dios los omnes perfectos,
> por que demuestran diuerssos ojetos
> aquellos que byuen en grant vana gloria;
> por ende propongo con sana memoria
> de dar mi sentençia syn otra reuista
> que de çynco ssesos mejor es la vista:
> asy la pronunçio por mas perentoria.
> (3.377)

Such stress on the visual emphasizes again the importance placed on physical appearance and attraction in courtly love; the judge's response misses the fact that the essence of enduring love is common attitudes and goals in life which can only be discovered through conversation.

The impression one receives from such debates is that the questions are tossed about more for the purpose of mental exercise in dispassionate analysis than in an attempt to assuage human despair or to understand human relationships. There is at least one problem, however, which does seem to imply a real dilemma of loyalty:

> Doctor . . .
> . . . .
> vn leal amigo con buena entençion
> dexó a su amiga en guarda de mi,
> la qual yo amaua sobre quantas vy
> e nunca le dixe aquesta rrason.
> . . . .
> en aqueste casso que deuo faser.
> (Fray Diego de Valençia, 3.498)

The question of whether the poet should follow his emotions or his conscience is the type of difficulty more likely to be encountered in life than those dealt with above. It is not a problem constructed on technicalities; if invented by the poet, it is certainly a dilemma in which a reader can imagine himself.

Despite the extensive conventionality and *lieux communs* of the *Cancionero de Baena* lyric, there are some unique features in the portrayal of women by these court poets. One unusual feature of the collection is that love in the context of marriage is not out of the question. Indeed this may be a continuation of the emphasis placed on conjugal love in the epic, an emphasis which seemed to reveal an important value of Spanish culture. Several poems in the collection are dedicated to a wife at the request of her husband; and she is portrayed within the courtly stereotype of female virtues even though at the time of the creation of this convention in southern France such qualities were attributed only to a lover, never to a wife. Villasandino wrote one poem in praise of the wife of a Señor Mayor in which he describes Señora Mayor in the following manner:

> Mayormente con su gesto
> e su bryo muy donoso,
> me fase beuir pensosso
> en plaser con todo aquesto;
> su fablar graçioso e onesto
> el mi coraçon vençio,
> quanto más que conteçio
> grand miraglo señaldo.
>
> (1.5)

Another poem of Villasandino, dedicated to a Doña Beatris for her husband the Infante D. Ferrando, clearly uses the same conventions of woman worship used in troubadour lyric, with the addition of Petrarchan comparison of the beloved with the cosmos:

> Amor me demostraste vna/señor que tan ben paresço;
> entre todas rresplandeçe/commo el sol ante la luna.
>
> (1.32)

Elsewhere in the poem she is compared to the "lus de parayso" and her face is termed "angelical." There is at least one poem, however, which does not portray a wife in accordance with the courtly stereotype. In this case Villasandino denounces his spouse for infidelity, a fault not only in the courtly ideal of a mistress but also in the Hispanic ideal of a wife: "Por ser leal rresçibo mal/donde plaser atendya" (1.6).

While the *Cancionero* contains a number of songs dedicated to the Virgin, Mary is not portrayed in the courtly manner of Alfonso el Sabio's *cantigas*. Rather, these songs convey a purely religious form of worship and service, for example:

> Madre de Dios verdadero,
> Vyrgen santa syn error,
> oyas a mi, pecador,
> que la tu merçed espero.
> . . . .
> rruega por tu seruidor
> pues ante nuestro Señor
> non syento tal medianero.
> (Pero Veles de Guevara, 3.317)

Villasandino also views the Virgin in the light of her protective and redemptive qualities:

> Tu me guarda noche e dya
> de mal e de trybulança.
> Ave Dei, mater alma,
> llena byen como la palma,
> torna mi fortuna en calma
> mansa, con mucha bonança.
> Inuyolata permansiste
> quando Agnus Dei paryste;
> fasme que non byua tryste,
> mas ledo syn toda errança.
> (1.2)

Such poems as these bear more resemblance to prayers written for recitation during a religious service than to lyric worship of a feminine ideal. In the *Cancionero* Mary is praised for her protective and motherly qualities, not for her ennobling powers and unreachable superiority. She is the mediator between man and God for man's redemption from sin.

Some critics believe a unique feature of the Spanish troubadours is that they place greater stress on personal involvement with their ladies and less on exterior beauty than did the Provençal poets. Our study has revealed that the poets revere physical beauty but do not tend to describe it in detail. On the other hand, their relationships to the ladies about whom they write do not come across as any more sincere or involving than those of the Provençal poets, even though the Spanish poets do mention the name of a specific lady in the titles of their poems more often than their Provençal counterparts do. One poem in which we could judge the emotions to be rare and personal is Juan Rodríguez del Padrón's poetic declaration of farewell to his lady written as he prepares to enter the priesthood. Escaping the convention of the day Padrón spends no time describing the lady's physical appearance. Rather the poem is a sad and sentimental, but certainly heartfelt, expression of his grief and wishes for her:

> Byue leda, sy podras
> non esperes atendiendo,
> que segunt peno sufriendo
> non entiendo
> que jamás
> te vere nin me veras.
> . . . .
> El trabajo perderas
> en aver de mi mas cura.   (3.470)

The forthrightness of this farewell and the lack of conventional woman worship certainly suggest that this poet is expressing his own sincere involvement and deep affection. Nonetheless his language is somewhat conceptual, and his use of the present participle reminds us of the style of Garcilaso and other Spanish poets of the next century.

Villasandino approaches the expression of sincere feeling in one poem, though the genuine sound of his declarations results from the fact that the situation is a purely Hispanic one which, no doubt, did occur often in the Middle Ages: the forced separation of lovers because of religious conflict. His description of the lady in question begins in the conventional physical terms:

> De asseo noble, conplido,   '
> aluos pechos de crystal,
> de alabastro muy broñido . . .
> (1.31 bis)

However, the fact that the girl is Moorish places the situation beyond that of the artificial troubadour context and into the world of conceivable reality where true dilemmas of the human condition are involved:

> Quien de lynda se enamora,
> atender debe perdon
> en casso que sea mora.

Criticism of women is a theme which brings out honesty and crude sincerity in the poets of the *Cancionero*. Several lyrics deal with a woman's unfortunate appearance or habits, and because such a straightforward portrayal contrasts sharply to the *lieux communs* of female beauty the effect is rather comic. Fray Diego de Valençia singles out one particular woman as a representative of a type of life repugnant to Hispanic morals:

> Segunt la vida que fases
> non menguas nada de puta;
> escuderos e rapases
> te fallan muy dissoluta,
> ca non han por nueua fruta
> de te provar a las veses.
>   (3.499)

For once we have the feeling that here is an individual woman who stands apart from the crowd because her qualities are not those attributed to all the others. Indeed it is almost a relief to find such comically harsh words addressed to a heretofore idealized being.

Velez de Guevara has also written an amusing poem to an ugly woman of noble lineage:

> Heu por que veio nuestra ssoedade
> veños vos esto, señora, a diser:
> vos non querades en al contender
> sy non en esto por vosa bondade
> que sy por esto non fore, sseñor,
> nunca creades que entendedor
> moyra de amores por vosa beldade.
>   (2.322)

In this poem *esto* refers to her noble lineage. The words *sseñor* and *entendedor* can be recognized as those used in the courtly convention, yet such frankness on the part of the poet, implying that only her title will win her a mate, makes us feel that this woman is truly of flesh and blood, an imperfect and real human being treated as such by man. It is interesting to note that if these poems imply an antifeminist tone, it is the first time this has been encountered in Spanish epic and lyric poetry of the Middle Ages. Such a current was widespread in the Spanish prose of the period as well as in the *Mester de Clerecía* narration of the *Libro de Buen Amor* and in Gallego-portugués *cantigas de escarnio y maldecir*, but has not been found in the Spanish epic and lyric poetry under study.[46]

Another type of poem also creates the feeling that the woman portrayed is of *carne y hueso* showing true emotions rather than a cold façade. Such is the case in a dialogue between Fernán Sánches Talavera and a former lady friend. While the lady used to believe the poet's declarations of love, she now makes it quite clear she will have none of him:

[El].   Mucho vos veo ser flaca.

[Ella].   Non curedes de la vaca,
           que no avedes de comer.

[El].   Seria ledo en vos ver
           bien alegre e plasentera.

[Ella].   Yd, que non soy la primera
           que fue loca en vos creer.

           . . . .

[Ella].   ¡Ay amigo! é no de poco
           amar a quien non vos ama;
           farta soy de mala fama.

[El].   Señora, mas non por mi!

[Ella].   ¡Ay señor Dios, ansy
           arda en fuego vuestra alma!
                              (3.537)

This dialogue portrays a woman of energy and spirit, a woman who emerges as an individual with personality amid a sea of expressionless faces. Her resentment is clearly true to human nature, his feigned innocence transparent. The result is the portrayal of an experience which affects us emotionally and makes us rejoice that for once a woman rejects her lover for just cause and not because such were the rules of courtly convention.

Comparison with popular lyric clarifies some apparent inconsistencies in learned lyric attitudes toward the female sex. While the popular lyric often centers on woman's sensual longings, the learned lyric does not discuss *her* desires but goes into detail in emphasizing woman as an object of physical love for man. The very thorough and sensually worded descriptions from head to toe are obviously written by men for men. Similarly the lyric critical of women is also written for the enjoyment of the male sex. On the other hand, the popular lyric views feelings more frequently from the feminine side and reveals neither supreme idealization nor gross criticism.

Furthermore, woman in the popular lyric is depicted in a greater variety of roles than is her more sophisticated counterpart of the upper classes; she is a daughter, a lover, a shepherdess, a happily or unhappily married wife, or a mother listening to her child's dilemmas and desires. In peninsular learned lyric, despite some appearances as a wife she is almost always cast in the role of lover, whether for praise or as an object of ridicule. Since the aspects of the noblewoman's life portrayed in learned lyric are very limited, descriptions of them naturally tend to be polarized.

While the emotions expressed in traditional lyric tend to be simple, human feelings which most women have experienced, and which therefore ring true, the complexity of form and language, the conventionality of metaphor and adjective in the majority of the learned lyric render woman a cold, almost dehumanized idol, a symbol rather than a truly warm human being of flesh and blood. Only the lyric of mockery removes her from this plateau. Indeed, one might say that more sincere esteem is shown for her in the epic and popular lyric, for here she is not limited to the role of playmate in a literary game or object of burlesque but rather is accorded respect in numerous roles. Despite the seeming reverence with which aristocratic woman is viewed, the poems of ridicule show us the other side of the coin. Beyond courtly games it is obvious that woman did not become the complete master in masculine-feminine relations.

On the other hand, we should not dismiss lightly the fact that, notwithstanding the influence of the European tradition on Spain's learned lyric, to some extent her poets did adapt the troubadour attitude toward woman to their own unique cultural environment. We have noted the retention of certain elements of the Hispanic popular tradition in such learned lyric as the *Razón de amor*, the *serranillas* and glosses of traditional *villancicos* by the Marqués de Santillana, the *cánticas de serrana* by the Arcipreste de Hita, the mention of conjugal love in the *Cancionero de Baena,* and even the frequency of dark eyes in all the lyric. The values or characteristics of the common people are rarely completely absent from Spanish literature.

Chapter Six

Conclusion

Our observation of the portrayal of woman in medieval Spanish epic and lyric poetry has revealed both the early view of woman in the formative years of medieval society as portrayed in the epic and also the development of this view as new social mores evolved. In the early epic poems we found that woman played a prominent though certainly not a central role in the narrative action. Her importance as a wife and mother, the stress on conjugal love, and the extremely high value placed both on her own honor and on the effect of her conduct upon the honor of her husband or parents showed that though woman was a subordinate being in a ruling masculine society, her moral judgment was a key factor within the family structure of the home. In terms of personality, epic woman was self-reliant and often self-assertive in the defense of her honor or her rights as she viewed them, and the epic poems were concerned more with her ethical choices than with woman as a "feminine" personality.

Emphasis on woman's physical beauty, her interest in clothing, her emotions, and her sentimental attachments was noted only in the subsequent ballads, particularly the erudite ones, and the presence of these new elements resulted from a change in society which had affected the literary view of woman. The epic had been primarily a masculine literary genre portraying the heroic world of feudal conflicts. In such a world woman had to be self-reliant, for man was often away. Even at home he apparently had little time or inclination to indulge any female desire for niceties, whether in goods or manners.

The popular lyric emphasized different aspects of woman's social role. Here she was of central importance, and the poetry revolved principally around her feelings rather than about epic action. Though her role with respect to the unique Hispanic concept of honor was not stressed as it was in the epic, nonetheless woman was still viewed as subordinate to man and dependent on him for her happiness. Yet while the epic stressed marital love and rarely introduced sensuality, the popular lyric did introduce woman in the role of lover with physical desires. Certainly, as in the epic, the Castilian and Gallego-portugués popular lyric presents her as a wife (happily or unhappily married) and as a sympathetic or cautious mother; yet it also introduces illicit relationships which would have been frowned upon in the epic. Under the probable influence of the Arab view of woman (as shown in the *kharjas*), the northern popular lyric finds her expressing the incipient sexual urges of youth or longing to be with her lover. Yet even though the emphasis is not on married love here, neither is adultery clearly indicated, and sensuality is expressed in a subdued manner. Judging by the greater freedom exercised in portraying woman's sentimental attachments and physical desires it is clear that the traditional lyric views the nature of femininity differently from the epic; still, we have found the kinship of the epic and popular lyric of northern Spain evident in the clear impact of the region's moral system on the portrayal of woman in both genres.

A radical change in woman's role in the social structure can be seen through her portrayal in learned lyric poetry. The two genres we have just considered, both popular in origin, seemed to present a varied and realistic picture of woman's several roles in the family and in society. Yet the erudite lyric not only centers totally on woman, but almost always views her in one fixed social position. Woman is now superior to man, regarding him with dispassionate disdain while he serves her hopefully but often fruitlessly. Even her physical appearance, stressed to a much greater extent than in epic or popular lyric, is regulated by convention. Now essential are aristocratic bearing, refined elegance, pristine, goddesslike beauty, courtly manners and learning—all qualities absent from the epic and traditional lyric. The extent to which this learned lyric portrayal of woman's personal qualities and relationship to men was realistic in terms of the society of the day is clearly questionable. Certainly it applied in real life to only a small minority of the populace, the aristocracy of the courts. The less stereotyped, more popular poetry written by poets such as Juan Ruiz and the Marqués de Santillana rounds out our view of what women were like at the time.

It is important to note that even within the bonds of convention the Spanish learned lyric maintains a unique flavor with respect to women when compared to the erudite lyric of other countries. While the ballads of King Rodrigo clearly bear the influence of courtly love's

woman-worship and Renaissance sensuality, the influence of the northern Hispanic moral system is also evident in the ballads as they maintain
the theme of rape and restoration of honor. This is clearly the northern
viewpoint, the Christian view, for such a theme is not present in the
kharjas of southern Spain.

Other examples of the retention of a strongly Hispanic view of
woman in the learned lyric should not be ignored. We saw, for example,
that the *serranillas* by Juan Ruiz present a special breed of mountain
girl quite distinct from refined *pastorela* types. Furthermore, in the
Cancionero de Baena, containing the purest examples of courtly love
lyric, we find the special imprint of the Hispanic view first found in epic
poetry: the clear presence of conjugal love is maintained as husbands
commissioned poets to write in praise of their wives.

The fact that the transition from the epic to the ballads and learned
lyric shows a change in woman's social status from the eleventh to the
fifteenth centuries does not prove that such was the case in all social
class levels. All genres reveal an elevated interest in woman's femininity,
but judging from the popular aspects we noted in the portrayals of
women in the *Razón de amor*, the *villancicos* and *serranillas* of Santillana, the *cánticas de serrana* by Juan Ruiz, the erudite imitations of
popular lyric in the Gallego-portugués *Cancioneiros*, and the *Cancionero
de Baena*, it is evident that among people of the more rustic society and
of the middle classes woman remained basically subordinate to man.
Probably in matters other than love this was also the case among the
aristocracy as well. Though she may have shed some of the assertiveness
brought on by the need for self-reliance in the feudal period, there is no
doubt that woman's social role remained important principally within
the context of marriage and family as the centuries passed. Certainly
this is the ideal presented in the epic and to some extent in the popular
lyric. In the learned lyric each poet dedicated love poems to many
women, normally a clear indication of a lack of the permanence or stability in male-female relations so important in the epic and popular
lyric. Nonetheless, we noted that most of the women to whom the
Spanish learned lyric was dedicated were either single women or wives,
so that Provençal stress on the adulterous nature of the relationships is
eliminated. Thus the stress in erudite lyric was not on the illicit nature
of the relationship any more than it was in the popular lyric. In all the

genres under study we find the stamp of a medieval Spanish cultural
pattern which frowned upon conjugal infidelity and viewed woman's
role principally within the family context. The epic and lyric of peninsular origin reveal that this pattern stresses not her beauty so much as
her behavior in relation to ethical codes.

Throughout this study the respect shown for woman has remained
almost constantly at a high level. Whereas much medieval prose and
poetry contained lewd mockery of woman's traditional faults in an
abundance of antifeminist literature, we have noted very little ridicule
of woman in the poetry under present consideration. Rarely was the
conjugal relationship criticized. Though the Arcipreste de Hita did ridicule woman, in essence his mockery was not based on an antifeminist
attitude. Rather it was an attempt to burlesque the portrayal of woman
in certain genres of his time, as we have seen. The mockery evident in
some poems of the *Cancionero de Baena* was as much a reaction to over-
idealization as a criticism of women per se.

Thus the epic and lyric poetry of medieval Spain reveal a culture
which respected woman more for her loyalty and admiration for man
than for her physical beauty. The popular lyric of the north, representing a genre with characteristics which are distinct from those of the
narrative epic, reflects the influence of Moslem values, showing the
sensual aspect of woman absent from the epic, while maintaining the
values of motherhood and family. The learned lyric, under the influence of European upper class courtly mores, shows that aristocratic
society veered somewhat from these values of Hispanic culture and
came to place more importance on female potential for refinement and
physical beauty. Yet even the erudite poets did not abandon the heri-
tage of Spain's unique respect for woman.

Notes

Chapter 1

1. Pierce Butler, *Woman*, vol. 5, *Women of Medieval France* (Philadelphia: George Barrie & Sons, 1907), pp. 11, 16-17.
2. Friedrich Heer, *The Medieval World*, trans. Janet Sondheimer (New York: New American Library, 1962), pp. 263-65.
3. Ibid., p. 265.
4. Information here relating to peasant women was based on Butler, *Woman* 5:17-18 and William Stearns Davis, *Life in a Medieval Barony* (New York: Harper and Bro., 1923), pp. 258-68.
5. Details of medieval education are based on Davis, *Life in a Medieval Barony*, pp. 26-27, 72-73, 82-84.
6. See Heer, *Medieval World*, p. 265 for more information on the anti-feminism of SS. Thomas Aquinas and Jerome.
7. H. A. Smith, "La femme dans les chansons de geste," *Colorado College Studies* 9 (1901):18.
8. Marc Bloch, *Feudal Society*, trans. L. A. Manyon (Chicago: University of Chicago Press, 1961), p. 136.
9. Unless otherwise noted, information gathered here about women in medieval Spain is based on Gonzague Truc, *Historia ilustrada de la mujer* (Madrid: Idea, 1946), 1:166-67, 231-33.
10. Details of Germanic family life are based on H. M. Gwathin and J. P. Whitney, eds., *Cambridge Medieval History* (Cambridge, Eng.: Macmillan, 1913), 2:631, 652.
11. Conclusions about women under Moslem rule are based on Claudio Sánchez-Albornoz, *España y el Islam:* "La mujer española hace mil años," pp. 91-97; E. Lévi-Provençal, *Histoire de l'Espagne Musulmane*, 3 vols. (Paris: G. P. Maisonneuve & Compagnie, 1953) 3:399-410; and García de Valdeavellano, *Historia de España: De los orígenes a la baja Edad Media* (Madrid: Revista de Occidente, 1952), 1:981.
12. Luis Gonzalvo, *La mujer musulmana en España* (Madrid, 1906), pp. 13-14 and Altamira y Crevea, *Historia de España y de la civilización española* (Barcelona: J. Gili, 1913), 1:287-88.
13. Sánchez-Albornoz, *España y el Islam:* "La mujer española," pp. 141, 118.

Chapter 2

1. This and subsequent verse citations are based on the text of Ramón Menéndez Pidal, ed., *El Poema de Mío Cid*, 10th ed. (Madrid: Espasa-Calpe, 1963).
2. J. Vicens Vives, ed., *Historia social y económica de España y América* (Barcelona: Teide, 1957), 1:343.

3. Citations from the two legal codes, *El código de las siete partidas* and *El fuero real*, will be given in three parts. For *Las partidas* the citation will give the *Partida*, the *Título*, and then the *Ley*. *El fuero real* is found in *Opúsculos legales del rey Don Alfonso el Sabio* (Madrid: Imprenta real, 1836) and the citations refer to the *Libro, Título*, and *Ley* in that order.

4. The *Fuero Real* ruled that if one marital partner died, the survivor kept half the property of the union while the heirs of the deceased retained the other half. See *Opúsculos legales* (3.1.1).

5. Truc, *Historia ilustrada de la mujer*, (Madrid: Idea, 1946), 1:172.

6. Claudio Sánchez-Albornoz, *España un enigma histórico*, 2 vols. (Buenos Aires: Editorial sudamericana, 1962), 1:618; Menéndez Pidal, ed., *Poema de Mío Cid*, p. 75.

7. Truc, *Historia ilustrada de la mujer*, pp. 129, 178.

8. Such inequality in viewing adultery is not confined to medieval Spain; in Roman, Jewish, and some American law, adultery is the title of a crime only when the woman participating in the act is married to a third person. If a married man and an unmarried woman have sexual relations this is not considered a crime of the grade of adultery. See Henry Campbell Black, *Black's Law Dictionary* (St. Paul, Minn.: West Publishing Co., 1951), p. 71.

9. An interesting modern incident of continued concern for masculine honor can be found in the criminal law of Texas. Article 1220 of the Texas Penal Code provides: "Homicide is justifiable when committed by the husband upon one taken in the act of adultery with the wife, provided the killing takes place before the parties to the act have separated. Such circumstance cannot justify a homicide where it appears that there has been, on the part of the husband, any connivance or assent to the adulterous connection." Texas courts have concluded that this section does *not* justify the wife in killing her husband's lover when she finds them under similar circumstances. Reed v. State, 123 Cr. R. 348, 59 S.W. 2d 122 (1933). Further, under Texas law if a husband learns that his wife has been killed, and in a state of rage, the husband kills the person responsible for his wife's death, the husband would be guilty of nonjustifiable homicide, although the penalty would probably not be severe. Article 1257b of the Texas Penal Code. It would thus appear that Texas law encourages a husband to value his own honor over his wife's life, considering the fact that he is treated leniently after committing homicide in a case where adultery is involved, but punished when he merely takes mortal vengeance against his wife's murderer. In view of the Hispanic code of honor it does not seem unreasonable to state that the Spanish tradition in Texas may account for the statutes.

10. See Ramón Menéndez Pidal, *La leyenda de los Infantes de Lara*, 2d ed. (Madrid: Imprenta de Librería y Casa editorial Hernando, 1934), p. 22 for a detailed account of available sources for the legend. Unless otherwise noted all page citations for quotations to follow refer to Ramón Menéndez Pidal, ed., *Primera crónica general de España* (Madrid: Gredos, 1955), vol. 1.

11. Ramón Menéndez Pidal, *La epopeya castellana a través de la literatura española* (Madrid: Espasa-Calpe, 1959), p. 69.

12. Ramón Menéndez Pidal, *Romancero tradicional de las lenguas hispánicas* (Madrid: Gredos, 1963), 2:5-6. Citations for quotations in this section refer to Alonso Zamora Vicente, ed., *Poema de Fernán González* (Madrid: Espasa-Calpe, 1953).

13. Information on the origins of the *Condesa traidora* legend is based on Ramón Menéndez Pidal, *Romancero tradicional de las lenguas hispánicas*, 2:255

and *Historia y epopeya,* in *Obras de R. Menéndez Pidal* (Madrid: Imprenta de Librería y Casa editorial Hernando, 1934), 2:11. In the latter Menéndez Pidal indicates that the *Chronicle of el Toledano* includes only the epilogue to the legend and that this version is slightly less cluttered with novelesque incidents than that of the *Primera Crónica.* Otherwise it contains no significant differences.

14. Ramón Menéndez Pidal, "Relatos poéticos en las crónicas medievales," *Revista de Filología Española* 10 (1923):337-38.

15. Ramón Menéndez Pidal, *Romancero hispánico . . . : Teoría e historia,* 2 vols. (Madrid: Espasa-Calpe, 1953), 2:265.

16. Truc, *Historia ilustrada de la mujer,* p. 236.

Chapter 3

1. See particularly Menéndez Pidal, *Epopeya castellana a través de la literatura castellana,* pp. 138-39. In addition, an analysis of all existing theories can be found in Menéndez Pidal, *Romancero hispánico,* vol. 1, chap. 2.

2. Discussion of the second epic poem here is based on Menéndez Pidal, *Epopeya castellana,* chap. 4.

3. Luis Felipe Lindley Cintra, ed., *Cronica geral de Espanha de 1344* (Lisbon: Academia Portuguesa de Historia, 1951), vol. 3.

4. Menéndez Pidal, *La leyenda de los Infantes de Lara* (Madrid: Imprenta de Librería y Casa editorial Hernando, 1934), p. 40.

5. Menéndez Pidal, ed., *Romancero tradicional de las lenguas hispánicas,* 1:3.

6. Quotations from the *Primera crónica general,* the *Chronicle of 1344,* and the *Crónica Sarracena* are from the text of Menéndez Pidal, ed., *Floresta de leyendas heroicas* (Madrid: Espasa-Calpe, 1958), *Rodrigo, el último godo,* vol. 1.

7. For a more complete analysis of the different versions of this poem see Raymond Grismer and Elizabeth Atkins, trans., *The Book of Apollonius* (Minneapolis: University of Minnesota Press, 1936), p. xii.

8. Stanza references are based on C. Carroll Marden, ed., *Libro de Apolonio* (Baltimore and Paris: Johns Hopkins Press, 1917).

9. Page references for ballads refer to Menéndez Pidal, ed., *Flor nueva de romances viejos* (Buenos Aires: Espasa-Calpe argentina, 1965) or to his *Romancero tradicional,* vol. 2.

10. Although C. Colin Smith in *Spanish Ballads,* (Glasgow: Pergamon Press, 1964), p. 92, states that the full-blown love of Urraca for Rodrigo derives from the second epic of the Cid legend, the *Mocedades de Rodrigo,* the supposed prose version of this epic in the *Chronicle of 1344* does not indicate but rather denies that any passion existed between the two. See the *Cronica geral de Espanha de 1344,* p. 298.

11. Menéndez Pidal, *La epopeya castellana,* p. 107.

12. Menéndez Pidal notes in *Poesía juglaresca y juglares* (Madrid: Espasa-Calpe, 1962) that the *Chanson de Roland,* written ca. A.D. 1040 numbers 4000 lines, that the *Chanson de Guillaume* (ca. A.D. 1080) counts 1938 lines merely in the first part, and that the *Charroi de Nîmes* (twelfth century) is 1450 lines long. These are much more extensive than the earliest Spanish epics, which are their contemporaries. Therefore Menéndez Pidal postulates that the French epic went through a period of development from shorter minstrel songs earlier than the Spanish epic. This would explain why France produced longer epics at an earlier date than Spain.

13. Américo Castro, *España en su historia* (Buenos Aires: Editorial Losada, 1948), p. 248.

14. George Fundenburg, *Feudal France in the French Epic* (Princeton, N.J.: Princeton University Press, 1918), p. 41.

15. H. S. Smith, "La femme dans les Chansons de geste," *Colorado College Studies* 10 (1903):38.

16. Bertha Louisa de Kok, *Guibourc et quelques autres figures de femmes dans les plus anciennes Chansons de geste* (Paris: Les Presses Universitaires de France, 1926), pp. 17-19.

17. Smith, "La femme dans les Chansons de geste," p. 8.

Chapter 4

1. For a more detailed analysis of the various types of peninsular traditional lyric than is included here see Dámaso Alonso, "Cancioncillas 'de amigo' mozárabes," *Revista de Filología Española* 33 (1949):310; Emilio García Gómez, "La lírica hispano-árabe y la aparición de la lírica románica," *Al-Andalus* 21 (1956): 314; Ramón Menéndez Pidal, "La primitiva poesía lírica española," in his *Estudios literarios* (Madrid: Espasa-Calpe, 1957), p. 260; and his *Poesía árabe y poesía europea* (Buenos Aires-México: Espasa-Calpe argentina, 1941), p. 62.

2. See Dámaso Alonso and José Manuel Blecua, eds., *Antología de la poesía española: Lírica de tipo tradicional* (Madrid: Gredos, 1964). The editors note (p. lxxxv) that while numerous poems in their collection are purely traditional, many others are developments on traditional poems by particular poets. Since the tone of both types is the same the authors have included both in their anthology, and we shall not distinguish between them in our discussion of their portrayal of woman. Another annotated collection of traditional peninsular lyric is José María Alín's *El Cancionero español de tipo tradicional* (Madrid: Taurus, 1968). Alín includes the earliest attested versions of many of the lyrics as well as later variants in the many cancioneros of Renaissance Spain.

3. For a detailed analysis of parallel form see Eugenio Asensio, *Poética y realidad en el Cancionero peninsular de la Edad Media*, (Madrid: Gredos, 1957), pp. 86-91.

4. S. M. Stern, *Les chansons mozarabes* (Oxford: Cassirer, 1964). A new edition and metrical study of the *kharjas* has been prepared by Emilio García Gómez: *Las Jarchas romances de la serie árabe en su marco* (Madrid: Sociedad de Estudios y Publicaciones, 1965).

5. Angel De Río and Amelia de Del Río, eds., *Antología general de la literatura española* (New York: Holt, Rinehart, and Winston: 1960), 1:4.

6. See García Gómez, *Jarchas romances* and Stern, *Chansons mozarabes*.

7. Menéndez Pidal, "*Primitiva poesía*," p. 251.

8. Peter Dronke, *Medieval Latin and the Rise of European Love-Lyric* (Oxford: Clarendon Press, 1965), 1:3.

9. Unless otherwise indicated all page references for *cantigas* cited will refer to texts included in J. J. Nunes, ed., *Cantigas d'amigo*, 3 vols. (Coimbra: Imprensa de Universidade, 1926), vol. 2.

10. Asensio, *Poética y realidad*, p. 56.

11. Alín indicates that the belt could also symbolize love (*El Cancionero*, p. 56).

12. Elza Pazeco Machado and José Pedro Machado, eds., *Cancioneiro da*

Biblioteca Nacional Antigo Colocci-Brancuti (Lisbon: Edição da 'Revista de Portugal,' n.d.), 2:297.

13. Menéndez Pidal, *"Primitiva poesía,"* p. 207.

14. Menéndez Pidal, "La primitiva lírica europea: Estado actual del problema," *Revista de Filología Española* 43 (1960):309

15. Dámaso Alonso, "Cancioncillas 'de amigo,' " pp. 344-46 and García Gómez, "La lírica hispano-árabe y la aparición," p. 320.

16. Emilio García Gómez, *Poemas arabigoandaluces* (Madrid: Espasa-Calpe, 1959), pp. 46, 48.

17. Ibid., pp. 83, 87.

18. Alonso, "Cancioncillas 'de amigo,' " pp. 336-37.

19. Asensio, *Poética y realidad,* p. 25. See also Dámaso Alonso, *De los siglos oscuros al de oro* (Madrid: Gredos, 1958), p. 32.

20. García Gómez, *Poemas arabigoandaluces,* p. 126; Martín de Riquer, trans., *La lírica de los trovadores: Antología comentada* (Barcelona: Escuela de Filología, 1948), 1:287.

21. See Leo Spitzer, "The Mozarabic Lyrics and Theodor Frings' Theories," *Comparative Literature* 4 (1952):1-22. Dronke, *European Love-Lyric,* p. 8, disagrees with Spitzer's suggestion that the "Man-song" of Provence originated from the so-called "Spring-song" though he does note that the origins of popular lyric in the Romance-speaking world may be found in the "Spring-song." See our chapter 5 for an examination of Dronke's theories.

22. Spitzer, "Mozarabic Lyrics," p. 17.

Chapter 5

1. Vicens Vives, *Historia social y económica,* p. 329.

2. Altamira y Crevea, *Historia de España,* 1:558.

3. Johan Huizinga, *The Waning of the Middle Ages* (Garden City, N.Y.: Doubleday Anchor Books, 1954), p. 108.

4. Maurice Valency, *In Praise of Love* (New York: Macmillan, 1958), p. 26.

5. Information on the courts of love and examples of disputes raised in them are taken from John F. Rowbotham, *The Troubadours and the Courts of Love* (London: S. Sonnenschein & Co., 1895), pp. 223-25, 249-50.

6. W. T. H. Jackson, "The *De Amore* of Andreas Capellanus and the Practice of Love at Court," *Romanic Review* 49 (1958):249.

7. See Dronke, *European Love-Lyric,* pp. 47-55 for a fuller explanation of his theory. Page references in our text pertain to this book. Dronke cites an article about courtly love by Mrs. D. R. Sutherland, "The Language of the Troubadours," *French Studies* 10 (1956) to support his suggestion that courtly love was not necessarily a platonic relationship.

8. Dronke, *European Love-Lyric,* p. 55.

9. Ibid., p. 48.

10. For greater detail on all of these theories see Dronke, *European Love-Lyric,* chaps. 1 and 2.

11. René Nelli, *L'érotique des troubadours* (Toulouse: E. Privat, 1963), pp. 192-95.

12. Charles H. Grandgent, *The Ladies of Dante's Lyrics* (Cambridge: Harvard University Press, 1917), p. 11.

13. Sánchez-Albornoz, *España, un enigma histórico,* I:413.

14. Guillermo Díaz Plaja, *La poesía lírica española* (Barcelona: Editorial labor, 1937), p. 52.

15. All of the textual quotations from the *Razón de amor* are based on the text of José M. Blecua, ed., *Floresta de lírica española* (Madrid: Gredos, 1963).

16. Leo Spitzer, "Razón de amor," *Romania*, 70 (1950): 151-53.

17. Menéndez Pidal, "Elena y María," *Revista de filología española* 1 (1914):52-53. Background here on the sources of this poem is based on his analysis, pp. 69-76. All line references for citations from the poem are from his text in this article.

18. Ibid., p. 69.

19. Discussion of Alfonso el Sabio's contacts with the troubadours and lyric of Galicia and Provence is based on José Amador de los Ríos, *Historia crítica de la literatura española* (Madrid: Rodríguez, 1863), 3:445-47 and 466. Further discussion of troubadour influence on Galician lyric can be found below in our treatment of the Marqués de Santillana.

20. All volume and page references for quotations from the text of the *cantigas* refer to the edition by Walter Mettmann, *Cantigas de Santa María*, 3 vols. to date (Coimbra: Por ordem da Universidade, 1959). The editor is preparing a fourth volume of literary and linguistic analysis which should prove useful.

21. Gonzalo de Berceo, *Milagros de Nuestra Señora*, ed. Antonio Solalinde (Madrid: Gredos, 1964), stanza 50, p. 13.

22. Aubrey Bell, "*The Cantigas de Santa María* of Alfonso X," *Modern Language Review* 10 (1915):342.

23. Unless other sources are noted, information on the origins and characteristics of the French *Pastourelle* is based on Alfred Jeanroy, *La poésie lyrique des Troubadours* (Toulouse: E. Privat, 1934), 2:282-91.

24. Edgar Piguet, *L'évolution de la Pastourelle du XIIe Siècle á nos jours* (Bern: Berthoud, 1927), p. 12.

25. Ibid., p. 11.

26. Page indications for troubadour lyric of Provence refer to Martín de Riquer, ed., *La lírica de los trovadores*, Antología comentada (Barcelona: Escuela de Filología, 1948).

27. Menéndez Pidal, "Primitiva poesía lírica," p. 230. Further information and discussion on the origins of the Spanish *serranilla* are based on this article, pp. 224-30 and on Pierre Le Gentil, *La poésie lyrique espagnole et portugaise à la fin du Moyen Age* (Rennes: Plihon, 1949), 1:534-40.

28. Le Gentil, *Poésie lyrique*, p. 541.

29. Ibid., p. 577.

30. Luciana Stegagno Picchio, "Per una storia della 'serrana' peninsulare: la serrana di Sintra," *Cultura Neolatina* 26 (1966):105-28.

31. Ibid., p. 109.

32. This and subsequent stanza references are based on the edition of Julio Cejador y Frauca, *Libro de buen amor* (Madrid: Espasa-Calpe, 1964), vol. 2.

33. Menéndez Pidal indicates that *luchar* in this sense is common to several Romance languages from the Latin *luctor*, referring to sexual fulfillment. See Menéndez Pidal, "Sobre la primitiva lírica española," in his *De la primitiva lírica española y antigua épica* (Buenos Aires: Espasa-Calpe argentina, 1951), p. 27.

34. Le Gentil, *Poésie lyrique*, pp. 630, 590.

35. Anthony Zahareas, *The Art of Juan Ruiz, Archpriest of Hita* (Madrid: Estudios de literatura española, 1965), pp. 148-52.

36. For other elements of parody here, see A. D. Deyermond, "Some Aspects

of Parody in the *Libro de buen amor*," in *"Libro de buen amor" Studies*, ed. G. B. Monypenny (London: Támesis, 1970).

37. Background references to Italian lyric of the fourteenth century are based on Robert A. Hall, Jr., *A Short History of Italian Literature* (Ithaca: Linguistica, 1951), pp. 67-105.

38. Vicente García de Diego, ed., *Marqués de Santillana: Canciones y decires* (Madrid: Ediciones de "La Lectura," 1913), pp. xix-xx.

39. From the text of Soneto 9 in Augusto Cortina, ed., *El Marqués de Santillana, Obras* (Madrid: Espasa-Calpe, 1964).

40. María Rosa Lida, "Notas para la interpretación, influencia, fuentes, y texto del *Libro de buen amor*," *Revista de Filología Hispánica* 2, no. 2 (1940):122.

41. Díaz Plaja, *Poesía lírica española*, p. 31.

42. Background information about the *Cancionero de Baena*, including general characteristics of its lyric and division of poetic generations is based on Rodolfo Ragucci, *Literatura medieval castellana* (Buenos Aires: Sociedad editora internacional, 1948), p. 203 and Rafael Lapesa, *La obra literaria del Marqués de Santillana* (Madrid: Insula, 1957), pp. 30-33.

43. Menéndez Pidal, "La primitiva poesía," pp. 210-11, 261.

44. Francisco López Estrada, *Introducción a la literatura medieval española* (Madrid: Gredos, 1966), p. 228.

45. Volume and poem numbers throughout our analysis refer to the textual versions in the three volume critical edition by José María Azaceta, *Cancionero de Baena* (Madrid: Consejo superior de investigaciones científicas, 1966).

46. For comparison one might consider a poem written in Gallego-portugués by Alfonso el Sabio. Though not contained in the *Cancionero de Baena* under study here, in its ridiculing attitude toward woman it does resemble those poems in the *Cancionero* of antifeminist tone:

> . . . .
> Non quer'eu donzela fea
> e velosa, como cam
> que ant'a mia porta peia,
> nem fata como alemã.
>
> . . . .
> Non quer'eu donzela fea
> que há brancos os cabelos,
> que ant'a mia porta peia,
> nem fata como camelos.
>
> . . . .
> Non quer'eu donzela fea
> veelha de ma coor
> que ant'a mia porta peia,
> nem fata e peyor.
> (*Colocci-Brancuti*, 2:333-34)

Typical of antifeminist lyrics, this poem describes woman as animalistic—hairy as a dog and producing excrement (the probable meaning of *peia*). The existence of this lyric may indicate that poets writing antifeminist lyrics in the *Cancionero de Baena* may have been influenced by similar *cantigas de escarnio* and *maldecir* in Gallego-portugués.

Index

CPSIA information can be obtained at www.ICGtesting.com
Printed in the USA
BVOW02s1347280715

410765BV00001B/36/P